Soul Reflections

Soul Reflections

Living a More Conscious and Meaningful Life

Diane Hancox, M.A.

Edited by Jan Freya

Order this book online at www.trafford.com
or email orders@trafford.com

Most Trafford titles are also available at major online book retailers.

Printed in the United States of America.

ISBN: 978-1-4669-0244-2 (sc)
ISBN: 978-1-4669-0245-9 (e)

Library of Congress Control Number: 2011919601

Trafford rev. 11/09/2011

 www.trafford.com

North America & international
toll-free: 1 888 232 4444 (USA & Canada)
phone: 250 383 6864 ♦ fax: 812 355 4082

Contents

Preface ix
Introduction...1
What Does It Mean to Be Self-Aware? 5
Moving toward Wholeness...9
What Lurks in Your Shadow? 13
The Healing Function of Soul.................................17
Soul Images..21
Our Inner World of Dreams....................................25
Projection Lessons..29
Your Ego Defends Itself 33
Facing Our Personas..37
To Be Normal or Not to Be Normal?....................41
Letting Go of Perfection...45
Journeying Through Life 49
Finding Your Own Path..53
What Are You Being Called to Serve?...................57
Finding Bliss 61
The Importance of Feelings....................................65
Learning to Be More Assertive..............................69
How Do You Handle Anger?...................................73
What Do You Really Need? 77
Fulfilling Your Needs 81
The Parental Imago in Our Relationships............85
Leaving the Childhood Home.................................89
We Are Complex in More Ways Than One 93
Choosing the Hero's Journey 97
The Cycle of Life...101

Depression Has a Role in Your Life 105
Archetypal Influences 109
Facing Adversity 113
When Fear Enters Your Life 117
Why Change Is Difficult 121
Learning to Make Good Decisions 125
Living with Uncertainty 129
Living with Fate 133
The Wisdom of Intuition 137
Abundance Versus Scarcity 141
The Importance of Gratitude 145
Afterwards 149
Bibliography 151
About the Author 155

Either you will
go through this door
or you will not go through.

If you go through
there is always the risk
of remembering your name.

Adrienne Rich

Preface

This book is a collection of articles that first appeared in the *Oceanside Star* newspaper in 2011 as part of a weekly column entitled "The Joy of Being Jung." Positive reader response encouraged the compilation of these thirty-six selections. Entries have been lengthened and revised, with reflective questions added to enhance the integration of topics and the personal growth in readers.

Immense gratitude goes to Brian Wilford, editor of the *Oceanside Star*, who initially offered me the weekly column and gave supportive feedback during copy submissions. Rebecca Coryell's encouragement was a constant throughout this (and other!) endeavor. The editor, Jan Freya, conducted a final review of the project, bringing both her editing skills and depth psychology knowledge to the book.

I acknowledge the works of Carl G. Jung, James Hollis, Marion Woodman, Joseph Campbell, June Singer, and James Hillman, among many who have written about the depths of the unconscious and the wisdom of psyche. I am appreciative of the knowledge gleaned through my M.A. experience at Pacifica Graduate Institute. Undoubtedly, nothing can compare to the personal learning received from my own ventures into my depths and also from the accompaniment of others whom are courageous enough to enter theirs. Thus, I thank Jungian Analysts, Douglas Cann and Greg Mogenson, and all the clients I have been honoured to work with over the years.

Introduction

A huge movement exists for us to find our true calling, to heal past wounds and to become more conscious as human beings. For the most part, however, we were taught to look outwardly for answers. We may keep hoping that the next job, partner, diet or wall colour will make us feel better, when in fact, the unconscious, our own inner wisdom, is where we need to go exploring.

Accessing the wisdom of the unconscious is an effective way to achieve these changes. *Soul Reflections* intent is to assist the voyage into the inner unconscious world for necessary reflection. These pages are intended to initiate an essential dialogue between the conscious and the unconscious, between the ego and the true self.

Our total beings or psyches are composed of both conscious and unconscious parts. The conscious parts are what we are aware of and know about. These include our routines, decisions, actions, relationships, urges and feelings. This is where the ego or 'I' lives.

The unconscious is the vast collection of thoughts and feelings that are hidden from our awareness. Why are they hidden? Very early in life, we learned which parts of us were designated 'not good,' and these were split off and repressed into the unconscious. We also learned which qualities were overvalued. Being cut off from the hidden parts results in the overuse of others, and our psyches become unbalanced. Fortunately, a psychic entity that Swiss psychoanalyst Carl G. Jung termed the *Self* observes both our conscious and unconscious worlds. The purpose of the Self is to maintain balance and the integration of psychic material.

The Self chooses qualities that need to be either incorporated or downplayed in order to create balance and move us towards wholeness. Additionally, the unconscious also reveals treasures—desirable qualities long ago chased into the darkness—waiting to enter joyfully back into our lives. In this way, the unconscious has a healing role necessary for overall wellness. The task now becomes working with our psychic material. The bizarreness of dreams, our spontaneous day fantasies, our body gestures, those interesting and sometimes embarrassing slips-of-the-tongue and those wondrous 'aha' moments as well as addictions, body symptoms and intense emotions all need to be viewed with a purposeful and symbolic lens.

Jung's concept of *individuation* and the possibility of self-metamorphosis are based upon wholeness rather than perfection and are attained through the reintegration of opposite traits into our consciousness. More often than not, our weakened egos hinder the acknowledgement of these traits. The work also comes in putting ego aside and, as Jungian Analyst Claire Douglas stated, honestly and willingly "confront and wrestle with the dark shadows and irrational forces beneath" our humanness.

The intent of your individuation is to establish personal responsibility that will jointly benefit the collective. As Jung stated, "the essential thing is the life of the individual . . . . Here alone do the great transformations first take place, and the whole future, the whole history of the world, ultimately spring as a gigantic summation of these hidden sources in individuals." In light of the political, economic, social and environmental turmoil that humans are currently facing, the urgency for personal and subsequent global transformation is at the forefront. As Jung further noted, if we in fact "make our own epoch," then there is no timelier place to begin than now.

You are invited to venture into the contents in no particular order in terms of chapters; however, the entries have been arranged from general concepts to those that are more specific, and in some cases, they have been clustered around similar topics. Although some of the reflection questions may seem repetitive, it is because they are key issues to address. I welcome you to use each reading and the subsequent reflection questions as a weekly focus or merely to open the book and see what area of your life comes up.

What Does It Mean to Be Self-Aware?

Socrates stated that the "unexamined life was not worth living." To examine our lives is to look at, observe and scrutinize what goes on both outwardly and inwardly. Today, we often call this *self-awareness*.

Self-awareness is the ability to look at and discern inner thoughts, feelings and beliefs. You could also say that self-awareness is being psychologically minded—being able to go beyond the surface of mere external happenings. Self-awareness involves entering the depths of your unconscious to look at your underlying beliefs and motives that determine your outer behaviour. You consciously and purposely ask, "What is really going on here?"

You can begin to increase self-awareness in a number of ways. Begin by taking responsibility for the situation and your feelings. Avoid external blaming or finger-pointing. Unless you are truly in a survival situation, no one has 'made' you feel or do anything. Did you really 'have to' do what you did, or were you reacting like you always have? Is that the way you really wanted to behave in that situation?

Start to look for patterns of feelings and behaviours. Do you tend to be emotionally triggered by certain people or in certain situations? On closer insight, you may find that you slip into expected or established roles such as the Good Daughter, the Super Organizer or the Poor-Me Child. You may find yourself acting in ways you would rather not. "Ah, there I go again! Why does this always happen (with my mother, co-worker or partner)?" What is really going on?

Situations that evoke strong or out-of-proportion reactions often indicate layers of both past and present feelings. In taking responsibility for the feeling, you might ask, "What am I so angry or frustrated about?" and "How am I angry at myself?" If as a grown person, you still feel at times like a little child when talking with a parent, ask, "How am I causing myself to feel like a dependent child?"

Self-awareness takes time, effort and the ability to take an honest and humbling look at yourself. Carl Jung stated that the *opus*—the work we do on ourselves—consists of three parts: insight, endurance and action. Insight is the awareness we bring to happenings in our lives. Endurance is being able to stay with the discomfort and pain of our suffering as we insightfully look at our shadow material. Finally, there is action—integrating and applying our learning into daily life and relationships.

Although becoming more self-aware is often seen as self-absorption, the resulting personal growth benefits more than the individual. As the 14th Dalia Lama stated, "I am going to use all my energies to develop myself, to expand my heart out to others, to achieve enlightenment for the benefit of all beings."

When we consciously reflect upon and take ownership of our feelings and behaviour, it takes us to a deeper, more meaningful level of relating with ourselves and with others. As Jungian Analyst and author James Hollis suggested, "during our time on earth, we all suffer. The choice is to suffer consciously or unconsciously." How will you start to examine your life?

Reflections

1. How comfortable are you with looking at your behaviour and taking ownership of your feelings and actions? Notice times when you have said, "He (or she or they) made me" either feel or do something.

———————————————————————

———————————————————————

———————————————————————

———————————————————————

2. What methods or tools do you use in your quest for self-awareness? In what ways or situations do you avoid looking at yourself? Spend some time reflecting upon why you evade these opportunities for growth.

———————————————————————

———————————————————————

———————————————————————

———————————————————————

3. Recall situations where you have done your opus or work. What were your insights? How did your endurance feel and look? How did the learning integrate into action?

———————————————————————

———————————————————————

———————————————————————

———————————————————————

4. Where have you suffered consciously? Where have you suffered unconsciously? What were the results of each type of suffering? What can you discern, conclude and advise about each type of suffering?

    _____

    _____

    _____

    _____

5. What role do you see self-awareness having in your life?

    _____

    _____

    _____

    _____

Moving toward Wholeness

We often hear the expression, 'We are born whole.' We search for wholeness and strive to be whole. We are born whole, with a balance of all the pairs of human qualities needed. Examples of such opposite traits include greed and moderation, productivity and idleness, and extroversion and introversion.

Early in life, however, we learned to value some traits and feelings more than other ones. Overt or covert messages such as 'Always be generous' and 'Never be lazy' may have been embedded into our psyches. We may have been told, 'Don't cry' or 'You're the responsible one.' This one-sided attitude splits the opposites, exiling some qualities, abilities and feelings into the unconscious while overvaluing others. When we are cut off from these hidden parts or overuse other, psychic imbalances occur.

Carl Jung called the collection of these hidden traits the *shadow*. These exiled parts of ourselves are usually deemed 'bad.' These qualities, however, are very much needed in our outer lives in order to maintain psychic balance, heal our early wounds, and lessen whatever amount of suffering we may have.

Recall that conscious material is the thoughts, feelings and actions in our awareness. The ego or 'I' is in charge of the conscious realm, as when we say, "I'm always punctual." If this is what ego believes, then the opposite quality, tardiness, will be avoided at all costs and is most likely found in the unconscious as shadow material. Tardiness will be seen as 'bad' and will probably evoke a strong reaction when we or others are late.

Our egos hold tightly onto certain roles and qualities with which they are comfortable with and have deemed 'good.' Outwardly, the ego appears strong, in control and believes it knows who we truly are; however, ego's defensiveness shows its apparent weakness and immaturity, as it is not strong enough to face (in this case) its own tardiness. The ego is not mature enough to say, "I accept that sometimes I can be late."

Jung used the term *Self* to refer to the part of the psyche which oversees both conscious and unconscious material. It shows us our imbalances through dreams, body symptoms and strong emotion. These serve as symbolic feedback of how the Self views the feelings, thoughts and behaviour under the ego's direction. It is as if a mirror is being held up to us saying, "Look. Here is what's really going on."

A dream, for example, reveals an image of a snail and the dreamer feels frustration. The Self might be showing the ego that feelings of frustration occur when things move slowly. The dreamer, who may outwardly be thinking, "Everything is okay," is inwardly and unknowingly frustrated.

If our egos are strong enough, they accept qualities and realizations about ourselves that humble us, making us more compassionate about how we view others and ourselves. When we encourage the ego to meet the Self, when we begin to take notice of our moods, gestures, dreams and body sensations, we are moving into an increased relationship with soul and towards wholeness.

<u>Reflections</u>

1. What messages infiltrated your childhood home as to how you were supposed to behave and feel? Name the traits that you learned to overvalue and undervalue?

   _____

   _____

   _____

   _____

2. How do you feel about the traits that you lost or that were undervalued? How might your life have evolved differently with those traits? How might these traits be integrated into your present life?

   _____

   _____

   _____

   _____

3. Think of a strong trait you have (e.g., responsibility, tidiness, art). Although no doubt being quite capable in this quality, was there some parental (or other) influence that may have enhanced your relationship with this trait?

   _____

   _____

   _____

   _____

4. What is your present relationship with your unconscious? How well do you notice your moods, gestures, dreams and body sensations?

_____

_____

_____

_____

5. Notice the times you say, 'I never . . .' or 'I always . . . .' These are opportunities to gain insights into shadow material. What are you denying you do that you need to own as part of yourself?

_____

_____

_____

_____

What Lurks in Your Shadow?

James Hollis recounted an old Near Eastern story of a man searching frantically for his lost keys under the light of a lamppost. A passerby attempted to help by asking, "Is this where you dropped them?" The searching man replied, "No, I lost them in the dark, but this is the only place where the light is." What is it about darkness that makes it so difficult to enter?

From a psychological perspective, the shadow is everything that makes you feels uncomfortable or embarrassed. Shadow is all that your ego does not want to know about or be. Shadow material is not evil or bad, and like the lost keys, it is useful and necessary. Carl Jung stated that to "confront a person with their shadow is to show them their own light."

Everyone has a shadow. Remember, in order to have basic childhood needs fulfilled, you had to overuse or underuse certain traits, beliefs and feelings. The undervalued ones were deemed wrong and were exiled into your unconscious, thus making you feel distressed when they are seen or experienced. If your persona proudly shows its qualities publicly, then your shadow hides opposite yet important traits.

This dualistic nature protects the ego and forms the basic of subsequent coping mechanism. This psychic division is no doubt reinforced by the Judeo-Christian doctrine that is based on the absolute value of good. Similarly, the Cartesian dualism philosophy emphasized a split of mind from body, polarizing consciousness and unconscious.

Shadow material is presented in a number of ways. One way is through the observations others make about you that surprise you. Someone may tell you, for example, "You're really creative," or state, "You seem to get upset when you talk about your brother." Your ego has difficulty with hearing about these traits and thus you may tend to discredit these remarks or even question the validity of them replying, "Really, I'm like that?"

Another signal that shadow material is present occurs when you deny, minimize or justify your behaviour. You may say, "I never lie" or "I'm not like that." Remember, you are born complete with all qualities and with both poles of opposing traits; however, taking ownership of these qualities is another matter. Notice the characteristics you have difficulty accepting, even in small amounts or in certain situations.

Shadow material is also exposed through projection. Projection occurs when qualities that you cannot admit in yourself are placed onto other people; for example, if you value a strong work ethic then you may find yourself repeatedly complaining about a co-worker's lack of dedication. Look for the presence of shadow qualities whenever strong emotions surface regarding another person.

Taking responsibility for shadow material challenges you to look humbly at who you are and the beliefs you live by. It further requires you to endure suffering when losses in persona and shifts in worldviews occur. Jung stated, "The shadow is a moral problem that challenges the whole ego personality, for no one can become conscious of the shadow without considerable moral effort. To become conscious of it involves recognizing the dark aspects of the personality as present and real."

When you face your shadowy elements this humanizes you, allowing you to be more compassionate and accepting of yourself and others. So, when looking for your lost keys, will you step into the darkness?

Reflections

1. Identify childhood qualities that were deemed 'bad' or were not valued by others in your family. How do you feel about these qualities? Are these traits and beliefs truly 'bad'?

    _____

    _____

    _____

    _____

2. What are some comments from others that you find hard to believe? Identify the traits that your ego is struggling to accept. What prevents you from realizing these qualities in yourself?

    _____

    _____

    _____

    _____

3. Notice when you use the phrases "I'm never like that" or "I'm always like this." Identify the trait you are overvaluing and the opposite trait you are not allowing yourself to experience. What would shift in your life if you let go of the overused trait and introduced the new trait?

_____

_____

_____

_____

4. Recall when you have integrated shadow material into your consciousness. What was the experience like? What did you have to let go of or accept?

_____

_____

_____

_____

5. How does acknowledging and accepting your shadow traits affect your relationships with others?

_____

_____

_____

_____

The Healing Function of Soul

As we watch television, we are bombarded with advertisements that claim to cure such ailments as anxiety, sleeplessness and depression. At times, we may opt for pain-relief medication to aid a headache. What are we really trying to cure?

From a medical perspective, to cure means that a patient no longer has the ailment. On the other hand, healing does not necessarily eliminate the disease; instead, it reflects a change in our attitude towards the complaint. This shift in perception may even extend to attitudes regarding other situations and people.

Depth psychology regards the psyche as the primary healer. Carl Jung used the term *metanoia,* from the Greek word, *metanoein,* meaning "to change one's mind" and "spiritual conversion," to denote psyche's attempt to heal itself. This may appear as a sudden 'nervous breakdown' or more slowly through chronic symptoms such as anxiety, depression, addictions and body symptoms.

Concerning neurosis, addiction or a symptom, Jung stated, "We do not cure it—it cures us." From this "purposive view," symptoms are not to be eliminated but are to be explored for their deeper meaning, as they "contain the true gold we should never have found elsewhere." If symptoms are treasures, they should not to be avoided or masked with medications. Underlying issues need to be explored and resolved rather than strengthened by existing coping mechanisms. Symptoms offer an opportunity for ego to ask, "What is psychically wrong or off?"

Jung valued not only the reality of the psyche, but also its wisdom and self-regulating function. He advised, "We must be able to let things happen in the psyche. Consciousness is forever interfering, helping, correcting, and negating, never leaving the single growth of the psychic processes in peace." Our egos, indeed, often act in opposition to what our souls desire by refusing to face our necessary shadow traits. Ego would rather rationalize and quick-fix its way out of symptoms; however, psyche will not give up its efforts towards wholeness and will not be silenced.

The word *heal* is rooted in *haelen* which means "to make whole or well," which is what psyche is seeking. Psyche interacts with ego in a compensatory way, striving for intrapsychic balance or homeostasis. Dreams and symptoms show inflations and deflations in opposition to the ego's one-sidedness. The intent of this psychic material is for us to adjust our egos' misguided beliefs in a compensatory and healing manner, leading us in an ongoing way towards the realization of our potential.

The principle purpose of psyche's self-regulation is changing our focus, attitude and values from an external locus to an internal one. In healing our symptoms, the implied responsibility is ours rather than solely the practitioner's. Start the process of healing by observing your body symptoms, patterns of moods, emotional triggers, projections, dreams and relationship issues.

Healing does not mean we reach an end-point where all will be perfect or fixed; rather, we achieve a better understanding of our inner conflicts, angst and suffering. We will continue to experience ailments and losses but will be better able to encounter them.

Eventually, as Jung suggested, we will consider a symptom with gratitude: "We should even learn to be thankful for it, otherwise we pass it by and miss the opportunity of getting to know ourselves as we really are."

<u>Reflections</u>

1. What is your relationship with your symptoms such as addictions, strong reactions to certain people or other neurotic behaviour? What do you think your symptoms are saying to you?

    _____

    _____

    _____

    _____

2. How well are you able to 'let things happen' in your psyche? To what extent does your ego get in the way of allowing psyche to heal itself?

    _____

    _____

    _____

    _____

3. How do you feel about the concept that psychic issues will never be cured, but rather are healed?

    _____

    _____

    _____

    _____

4. How well do you take responsibility for your ailments? Consider how much responsibility and power you give to doctors, mechanics, employers and others with whom you deal.

_____

_____

_____

_____

5. What wisdom have you learned via your symptoms? How would you advise others to glean their inner wisdom from their symptoms?

_____

_____

_____

_____

Soul Images

Whether you call it psyche, life force, or essence, the concept of soul is difficult to define. Regardless of a precise definition, however, soul is generally agreed upon as the source of meaning in one's life. Perhaps one reason the soul is difficult to define is that it does not originate from the usual process of right-brain linear thinking. Rather, the soul speaks or reveals itself through images.

According to Carl Jung, the soul or psyche consists essentially of spontaneous images. Thomas Moore, author of *Care of the Soul*, agreed, stating that images are the soul's "native language." Images come in the form of dreams, body gestures, intuition and metaphor. What about those sudden images or memories that appear throughout the day? If your conscious mind did not purposely think them up, then the creative source turns to the soul.

When you do not pay attention to these daily soul whispers, the soul turns the volume up. It now tries to get your attention through disturbing dreams, feelings of depression, addictive behaviour and chronic body distress. As the gap between how you are living and how your soul wants you to live increases, so does your suffering. The Sufi poet Rumi stated, "What hurts the soul most is to live without tasting the water of its own essence."

When you begin to take notice of your moods, gestures, dreams and body sensations, you are moving into relation with soul; however, one difficulty in working with the soul is that the messages often appear to make little sense.

This is because the soul speaks using symbols, feelings and metaphor. For growth to occur, the symbols need to be seen as constructive attempts of psychic change.

Try working with such images in an abstract way, much as you would art, poetry or music. Try to sense the overall feeling and theme of the image. The key is not to interpret or to solve, but to be curious and creative. Use, for instance, the image of your pet dog slowly sliding down a cliff while retrieving a stick, which leaves the dog perched in a fallen tree. This image could have been a dream or a waking image that flashed spontaneously into your awareness.

Hold the image. Notice any feelings (e.g., scared, panicky). What about any body sensations (e.g., heart pounding)? Make associations to your pet, such as joy, innocence, puppyness, or its name. Then observe the situation, which, in this case, could be 'over the cliff,' 'slippery slope,' 'out on a limb,' and 'too close to the edge.' Do the same with any actions (e.g., playing, fetching, and sliding).

Arrange the ideas in sentences. 'When I play too close to the edge, my joy gets stuck.' Alternatively, it could be 'I'm asking my loyalty to fetch something in a risky situation.' The challenge now comes by asking, 'Why is my soul sending me this image now?' In this case, the answer could be 'Where in my life am I compromising my joy, acting risky, or out on a limb?' Return to the feeling: 'What risky situation is truly making me panic?' When you are ready for a psychological change and ego has stepped aside, the humbling answer or insight will come.

Do not be concerned with whether you have figured out the image or not. The key is that you have honoured the image and attempted to 'taste the water' of your own essence. Trust that psyche will continue to give you images and other material for further exploration.

Reflections

1. How does your soul speak with you? Do you recall dreams readily? Does you body tend to speak to you through symptoms? Alternatively, do you tend to have addictive behaviour or patterns of dysfunctional relationships?

    _____

    _____

    _____

    _____

2. Note your use of metaphors or puns during the day (e.g., I feel like I'm carrying a ton of bricks.). Treat these statements as images and work with them symbolically (e.g., What part of me is weighing me down? How am I currently burdening myself?).

    _____

    _____

    _____

    _____

3. Begin a soul journal to record dreams, day fantasies, slips-of-the-tongue and situations that evoke emotive reactions. Here you can further process each happening and look for connections, themes and changes among them.

    _____

    _____

    _____

    _____

4. Looking at the contents of the unconscious is often very humbling. How willing are you to hear both the positive and suggestive material that soul offers you? Is your ego strong enough to admit its weaknesses?

_____

_____

_____

_____

5. When working with psychic material, give yourself permission to be playful. Enter the right brain realm of feelings, body sensations, creative movement, drawing, singing, not having to know, imaging and wonder.

_____

_____

_____

_____

Our Inner World of Dreams

Many people believe dreams are created by the brain randomly throwing together memories and recently experienced material. From a psychological perspective, dreams are created by the soul or psyche as a way of communicating to the dreamer. Psychoanalyst Sigmund Freud stated, "Dreams are the royal road to the unconscious." Carl Jung felt that "the dream is a little hidden door in the innermost and most secret recesses of the psyche."

Dreams show qualities of ourselves to be observed and either downplayed or incorporated more fully in order to create psychic balance and movement towards wholeness. These traits and beliefs are shown through events and the actions and feelings of dream characters. Marie Louise von Franz suggested asking, "What is it in me that does that?" As we take ownership and begin to integrate these traits into our daily lives, personal growth occurs, and new energy emerges.

Dreams are one way to gain insights into how we are journeying through life and act in self-regulating ways. Author June Singer noted, "The unconscious presents a point of view which enlarges, completes, or compensates the conscious attitude." In dreams, one's true self holds up a mirror and says, "This is my take on what's really going on." As James Hillman suggested, "the soul is ceaselessly talking about itself in ever-recurring motifs in ever-new variations, like music and it is immeasurable deep."

Most dream work begins with making associations to the dream characters and objects. Provide descriptive words or qualities for people, settings and objects in the dream. Are there any memories connected to these dream items? Try to capture the essence of each item in one or two words, such as 'young rebel' or 'wide-open field.' Actions in dreams, such as running, cutting, and deciding, can spark further associations. The act of cutting, for example, may lead to cutting through, cutting out, shearing, trimming, and dividing.

Another interesting approach is making comparisons to the dream material. What was an object in the dream *like*? 'It's *like* when . . .' or 'It's *as if* . . . .' This playful language works well with images. Say the dream aloud. Listen for puns, metaphors, and statements that provoke a reaction or emotion from you. Try to summarize the dream in one sentence, then in one word. Title the dream.

A key function of dreams is the processing of feelings. In the book, *Mindsight,* author Daniel Siegel stated that dreaming is "one of the important ways we integrate memory and emotion," with the dream serving as "an amalgam of memories in search of resolution." The feeling tone of the dream is more important than the actual content of the dream. Start by looking at the feelings felt by figures in the dream. How does the dreaming you and the waking you feel about the dream's events?

Honestly address the question, In what situation might I be experiencing (or deny experiencing) feelings similar to those in the dream?

Relate the feelings and the theme of the dream to current situations such as making a specific decision, an attitude or an emotionally charged situation. Remember, the ego is rarely pleased with unconscious material. Challenge your ego by asking, "What aspect of myself which is difficult to see or admit does my soul want me to know about?"

Reflections

1. What is your relationship with your dream life? Where do you think dreams come from? What do you think their purpose is?

    _____

    _____

    _____

    _____

2. When doing your dream work, note which parts of the dream you are negating, avoiding or focusing on. These actions often indicate ego's presence and its desire to focus on parts that appeal or please it. Challenge yourself to explore all parts of the dream, especially those that you are avoiding.

    _____

    _____

    _____

    _____

3. Try to relate the feelings and the theme of the dream to current situations such as making a specific decision or a conflict with someone. Challenge your ego by asking, "What aspect of myself that is difficult for me to see or admit does my soul want me to know about?"

    _____

    _____

    _____

    _____

4. Archetypal scholar James Hillman stated, "A dream tells you where you are, not what to do." Be conscious of ego's quest for wanting to find answers when working with your dreams. Ask yourself, "Why is my soul sending me this image now?"

    _____

    _____

    _____

    _____

5. What wisdom have you received from dreams?

    _____

    _____

    _____

    _____

Projection Lessons

You may often be fascinated by finding images in the shapes and textures of clouds. Is that the profile of Gandhi or a rabbit? The well-known Rorschach inkblot psychological test works in this manner. How do you get from that cluster of clouds or blob of ink to a distinct image?

When you see unrecognizable images, your conscious mind cannot logically figure them out. In order to make sense of the image, you use ideas that emerge mainly from your unconscious in a process called *projection*. The author Anaïs Nin succinctly described projection: "We don't see things as they are, we see them as we are."

Projection occurs when your unconscious feelings, qualities and thoughts are placed onto external people, situations and objects. Remember, unconscious material includes qualities that your ego does not appreciate as they do not fit with your ego's conception of who you are. Rather than take ownership of these qualities, out they go. "I'm not like that!" exclaims your ego. Because projection consists of unknown and disowned parts of you, awareness and reflection of projection can lead to great personal insights.

Take the example of being at a four-way stop and observing a driver doing a rolling-stop before proceeding through the intersection when there is no chance of hitting or harming anyone. You immediately feel angry and are in disbelief as to how someone might do this.

In working with the projection, start with any feelings that arise in you. In this scenario, it might be shock, resentment, and anger. Go further by asking yourself, "What specifically were these feelings about?" Possible replies to the resentment might be, "It's not fair!" or "How dare they not follow the rules."

Take the projection further back. Remember, if this is shadow material, you are either over or undervaluing the quality. Ask yourself, "Where in my life am I doing too much or not enough of this trait?" In this case, you might ask, "How do I follow the rules too much? Where am I breaking the rules and don't admit it?" Pay attention to the feelings. "Where I am feeling some unfairness? How am I being unfair to myself or to someone else?"

Throughout your daily interactions with others and even with your solitary tasks, projection shows the ego your unknown qualities. The strong reaction to the incomplete stop indicates the presence of shadow material. If your ego was comfortable with not following the rules sometimes or understood that sometimes life is unfair, then there would not have been such an intense reaction. Your ego might outwardly adhere to rules, but inwardly, unconsciously, your soul is letting you know, "Hey, that's not so bad. Let's try that once in a while."

Projection also occurs around qualities deemed favourable. You can enviously admire someone for their creative ability and yet not realize your own. Taking the projection back, ask yourself, "Where am I creative? In what aspect of my life do I need to introduce some creative energy?"

Partners, friends, co-workers and strangers evoke reactions in you in order to increase your self-awareness. Your task is to claim these projections. As the poet Anne Waldman wrote, "the problem with you is the problem with me." Carl Jung stated that to "confront a person with their shadow is to show them their own light." When you face your shadowy elements this action humanizes you, allowing you to be more compassionate and accepting of yourself and others.

Reflections

1. Which people tend to 'push your buttons' or make you upset or angry? Identify the quality in the person that bothers you. Take ownership of that quality. How are you similar to the person? How might you need to increase or decrease the quality in yourself?

    _____
    _____
    _____
    _____

2. Think of someone you admire. Identify the qualities in that person that you deem admirable. Take ownership of these traits. How do you view these traits in yourself? How might you be denying these traits?

    _____
    _____
    _____
    _____

3. Think of a situation (e.g., arriving late or spilling a beverage) that you have difficulty experiencing. Name the feelings that arise during the situation. Identify what traits or expectations you are projecting onto the situation.

    _____
    _____
    _____
    _____

4. Whether dealing with potential intimate partners or new acquaintances, a great deal of projected material is often placed onto others at the beginning of a relationship. This occurs because you unconsciously fill the lack of information about the person with traits, hopes and expectations you hold in your unconscious. Identify the material you have placed onto others to fill the void.

---

5. As you become better at noticing your projections, you will begin to notice when others are projecting onto you. Your task is first to notice the projection and then to be aware of the degree to which you accept the projected traits or role. Are you perpetuating the projection? Do you need to give the projection back to the person?

Your Ego Defends Itself

The ego is the centre of your identity and the part of you that you associate with when using the term "I." As a child, your ego developed by adapting itself to what was compatible with family and societal surroundings; however, this alignment came with a cost. In order to protect yourself from the hurt or rejection from others, you split off parts of yourself that were undervalued or even deemed 'bad. You instinctively accentuated parts of yourself that brought reward or praise and repressed other parts that, when expressed, were met with fear, shame, guilt or devaluation by caregivers. Coping or ego defense mechanisms were established in order to insure your safety by keeping these parts out of ego's recognition.

Repression is the primary way the ego protects itself. In this process, distressing and uncomfortable memories and feelings are kept from consciousness; however, these may later surface when triggered by certain situations. You may avoid or try to hide certain feelings and qualities you have. Your ego proclaims, "I just don't do math" or "I never cry." You may rationalize your actions by making self-serving explanations such as "That's the way I was raised."

You may use humor to avoid both external and internal conflict. From the way you are speaking, others might get the impression that you are good-natured and happy; however, this façade allows you to avoid voicing your true feelings. Feelings may even be nonexistent or isolated regarding a certain situation. You may find yourself intellectualizing, giving facts and statistics about your parent's medical condition and mentioning nothing about how you are feeling.

Through the process of projection, unacceptable feelings and traits are wrongly placed onto others. In an exaggerated form, projection results in others becoming idealized or becoming 'the enemy.'

Denial is another way to dispel anxiety-causing thoughts and feelings. In these situations, you refuse to acknowledge parts of yourself that are readily apparent to others. The surprised ego states, "I'm not like that!" Ironically, even positive qualities such as creativity and a sense of humor may be denied by ego's one-sided view of itself.

Not all defense mechanisms are 'bad' or unhealthy, as self-protection is needed when dealing with daily challenges. The key is moderation and awareness as to why you are using them. When distressed, you may cope by seeking the emotional or physical support of others. At others times, keeping an optimistic outlook may help shift your thinking to future situations and to consider realistic scenarios or solutions. Suppression is the conscious decision not to think about what is bothering you. Moderate suppression is healthy but, in excess, becomes avoidance.

The problem with defense mechanisms is that the thought or feeling does not disappear. Carl Jung stated, "What you resist, persists." In fact, the idea or feeling often intensifies and continues unconsciously to effect your decisions and reactions. A common example is the repression of disappointment or resentment finally showing up as angry outbursts. The task of the ego is therefore to become aware of the ways it handles its fears and discomforts. Ask yourself, "What is this coping behaviour trying to protect me from?" or "If I didn't do this behaviour, what might I have to face or do?"

Reflections

1. What parts of yourself do you keep away from ego's recognition? Notice your use of "I never" or "I always." Where did the devaluing of the traits or feelings originate?

_____

_____

_____

_____

2. Notice whom you idealize and whom you have made into an adversary or enemy. Identify the qualities you have disowned and placed onto others. Take ownership of these qualities by acknowledging where these traits show up in your life.

_____

_____

_____

_____

3. Denial, minimizing and rationalizing or intellectualizing are easily identifiable defense mechanisms. Try to be more aware of these throughout your day. What belief or trait are you trying to defend when using these tactics?

_____

_____

_____

_____

4. Begin to notice defense mechanisms in others. In this way, you can become more compassionate and empathetic to them and to yourself.

_____

_____

_____

_____

5. In what situations do you use healthy coping mechanisms? Are there some that you have a tendency to overuse?

_____

_____

_____

_____

Facing Our Personas

The actor Claire Danes wisely stated, "The life of my persona has nothing to do with me." What exactly is a persona? In Latin, *persona* originally meant a mask worn by actors to indicate the role they played. Carl Jung used the term *persona* to represent the 'I' that one presents to society. It is also the 'I' that society expects us to show it.

Like the theatrical mask, the persona gives an indication of what we are like. It helps define who we are, which is helpful and often necessary in social settings. In different situations, we put on different masks such as the Husband, Father, Son, Coach, Entertainer or Boss.

The persona is also useful in that it mediates between our true selves and society and acts as a protective covering. The persona, however, is actually a compromise between what we truly are and what society expects us to be. As with any mask, the traits exhibited are often deceptive and skewed in relation to what actually lies beneath the mask.

Neptune, the Roman god of the sea, is referenced as often being masked and is associated with deception, disillusion and seeing the world and ourselves through rose-coloured glasses, unaware of the shadowy truth. Similar to what lies behind our personas, the sea's tranquil surface deceitfully hides its underlying turbulence. What is the cost of our personal deception?

When we overly identify with a persona, we lose sight of who we are. We take on roles, complete with a set of rules, standards, 'shoulds' and 'musts' associated with each of them. We begin to act in a predetermined way according to expectations elicited by the role rather than in ways we truly feel and want to act.

When our egos are too attached to a persona, we lose sight of other aspects of ourselves. These neglected yet necessary traits remain further hidden or entrenched in the unconscious. Dreams and outer situations may start to present symbols of dress, armor, veils, masks and shields. Distinct roles such as Teacher, President, Server or Caregiver may also become more noticeable.

As we move farther away from our souls or true selves, a huge psychic division occurs. This may lead to loss of meaning, depression, emotional outbursts, increased body distress and addictive behaviours. As the division widens, we begin to feel trapped, stuck or crazy.

Midlife is a phase in life when persona is noticeably challenged. Upholding the roles of Super-Parent, Good Daughter, Loyal Supporter or Carefree Wanderer for decades may cause the soul finally to shout, "Enough!" We may reach a crisis, exclaiming, "I'm not going to do this anymore!"

As we leave the sea's calm surface and dive into the turbulent depths, we ask ourselves questions, perhaps for the first time: "Who am I?" and "How do I really want to live my life?" As Ralph Waldo Emerson stated, "to be yourself in a world that is constantly trying to make you something else is the greatest accomplishment."

In Italian, *per sonare* means "to sound through." Perhaps this is a more soulful way of looking at persona. Instead of wearing masks, we can strive to exist so the voices of our true selves come through.

Reflections

1. What labels or roles have been or are currently placed on you? How did these labels originate and who gave you these labels?

   _____

   _____

   _____

   _____

2. How do you feel about each of the identified labels? Recall how you felt when these labels were initially placed on you. How willing were you to accept these labels?

   _____

   _____

   _____

   _____

3. Look at each of the personas you fulfill. What needs are being meet by you and by others as you carry out each role?

   _____

   _____

   _____

   _____

4. Imagine current personas being partially or fully removed. How would this change shift your perception of yourself? How might this removal alter how you approach certain situations? How might this change affect others' perceptions and ways of relating with you?

---

5. Who are you? Imagine yourself without your job, your possessions and your status. What beliefs and values will still govern your life? What abilities and traits will you still possess and be able to offer?

To Be Normal
or Not to Be Normal?

At certain times in our lives, we state, "I feel like I'm going crazy." During these moments, we certainly do not feel our usual or normal selves, but what exactly does it mean 'to be normal'?

Norma, the Latin origin of the word *normal,* means "conforming to common or collective standards" or to what is "the usual rule or pattern." Interestingly, *normalis* refers to being made according to a carpenter's square or the ninety-degree 'right' angle. In statistics, the normal distribution is where the bulk of the results lie. We are conscious of collective normal behaviours when driving, conducting introductions and in making most decisions.

When one places too much concern on 'being normal,' imbalances occur. Carl Jung suggested that, "What passes for normality is often the very force which shatters one's personality or sense of self." In the act of trying to be 'normal' or socially acceptable, we often violate our inner natures and this act causes mental or psychological distress. As the writer Albert Camus stated, "nobody realizes that some people expend tremendous energy merely to be normal."

Although not commonly used outside of clinical settings, the term *neurotic* refers to any mental distress whose behaviour is within socially acceptable norms. (There's that term again!) Neurotic behaviour shows up as restlessness, addiction, anxiety, aimlessness, obsessive-compulsivity, anxiety, depression, anger, low self-worth, dependency, negativity and perfectionism. We all have neurosis and can learn from them.

Neurotic behaviour is a way of coping with some sort of psychological distress. Something is 'off' deep within oneself. Jung suggested, "People become neurotic when they content themselves with inadequate or wrong answers to the questions of life." Our souls see the gap in how we live our normal lives and how we truly want to live. Physicist Albert Einstein stated that we unconsciously drive ourselves insane by "doing the same thing over and over and expecting different results." We become the mouse on the wheel, endlessly going round and round.

The craziness and neurotic behaviour beckon us to take a deeper look at what is truly happening. We often begin to see patterns of unhealthy behaviour. We begin to question the beliefs or motives underlying our actions. A good place to start is to ask, "Has this way of thinking, believing or acting been working for me lately?" Although the ego will not like it, our souls will answer, "No. I want something else, something more meaningful and alive."

This 'something else' is usually found outside our normal ways of thinking; outside the too-long-lived set of rules and beliefs that dictate societal and family of origin norms. Ironically, we eventually, often painfully, realize that what is truly absurd or abnormal is living with too much normalcy. It is crazy-making to live 'like everyone else,' inside the box, denying what our souls want.

To be normal is to live according to what the soul feels is best. To live a meaningful life, you must at times be willing to think and behave counter to what the majority of people think and do. Like the carpenter, craft your life based upon your own 'right,' regardless of whether it is ninety-degrees or something else.

Reflections

1. What do you think is 'normal'? How were people who were 'not normal' viewed in your family of origin? How are people 'outside the box' treated in your workplace, family or community? What are your views or attitudes on 'being normal'?

    _____

    _____

    _____

    _____

2. Reflect upon times when as a child you tried something or did something 'outside the box' or different from the ways things were done in your household. What were the consequences of this behaviour? How did the consequences affect your subsequent behaviour?

    _____

    _____

    _____

3. How normal are you? In what situations do you feel normal and not normal? What internal messages do you give yourself in each of these situations? Whose values are these messages based upon?

    _____

    _____

    _____

    _____

4. Recall times in which you felt as if you were 'going crazy.' What were the two (or more) perceptions (voices, attitudes) that occurred or were creating an internal battle during these situations? Give each of these voices a name or title, for instance, The Protector, The Should-er.

———————————————————————————

———————————————————————————

———————————————————————————

———————————————————————————

5. Moving away from normalcy to living a life in greater accordance with your true self results in losses. Reflect upon the losses (job, money, status, friends, security, control) endured when you have done something more aligned with your self, yet different from others or the usual way you have conducted your life.

———————————————————————————

———————————————————————————

———————————————————————————

———————————————————————————

Letting Go of Perfection

In the film, *Black Swan*, the ballet director challenged Nina, the featured dancer played by Natalie Portman, by stating, "I never see you lose your self." He further explained, "Perfection is not just about control. It's also about letting go. Surprise yourself so you can surprise the audience."

Jungian author Marion Woodman provides one explanation for the need for perfection. She states that children become "superadjusted to reality," which manifests as being the good girl or boy, being charming and perfecting their performances. As much as this coping mechanism or adaptation fulfilled the needs of the parents (who, as Woodman suggested, "were not able to emotionally support the child"), the child paid a cost: parts of him or her self were lost or overly controlled.

In the book, *Depth Psychology and a New Ethic,* Jungian psychologist Erich Neumann explains another reason for the need for perfection. He points to an "old ethic," originating from Judeo-Christian and other sources, which is based on the absolute value of good and is achieved by "the elimination of those qualities which are incompatible with this perfection."

Both authors' explanations involve a denial of negative aspects of the self, which is accomplished by either conscious suppression, as in self-discipline and sacrifice, or by unconscious repression. Regardless, a splitting of the psyche occurs, with the ego deemed as absolute good or perfect and shadow as bad or imperfect. A personal wounding occurs in which genuine feelings and attributes of our selves are disowned, and we are thus left incomplete.

Being perfect, having control, being dutiful and constantly checking ourselves takes energy. Eventually, usually during midlife, the soul becomes weary of this performance. This weariness appears as a lack of energy or libido, sadness and anger, and through the introduction of chaos into our lives. After decades of willpower, control and striving for perfection, the compensatory nature of the psyche brings the opposite.

The task now becomes the "new ethic"—acknowledging, welcoming and integrating the once deemed 'bad' qualities into our consciousness. This integration of shadow material is part of the individuation process, the purpose of which, as Carl Jung explained, "is not perfection but completeness, and even that is well beyond the reach of most mortals."

Jung further stated that "one does not become enlightened by imagining figures of light, but by making the darkness conscious." The integration of our darkness is vital for our well-being. We are both good and evil, both heaven and hell, and both godly and satanic.

A helpful mindset to hold as we wrestle with our imperfections is informed by Jung's thought that *"imperfectum* carries within it the seeds of its own improvement." When we become aware and take ownership of our imperfections, we can enter into a more compassionate relationship with ourselves and others. Native American beadwork and Persian rugs are made with one intentional flaw to show that the artist was only human. The spirit bead, or the 'mistake' bead, acts as a gate through which the Great Spirit, or God, can enter the art.

Although having caught the only perfect game in World Series history, baseball catcher Yogi Berra wisely acknowledged, "If the world were perfect, it wouldn't be."

Perhaps it is time in your life to give up the need for the perfect game and accept some errors, wild pitches and runners-on-base.

Reflections

1. What is your relationship with perfection? How important was 'being perfect' in your childhood household? To what degree and in what areas was perfection expected?

    _____

    _____

    _____

    _____

2. How do you truly feel about your less-than-desirable tendencies or aspects such as greed, addiction or a physical feature? What messages tend to play in your mind about these traits? You were not born with these views. Where and from whom did you learn these?

    _____

    _____

    _____

    _____

3. When doing a task, challenge yourself to make an intention flaw. Note your feelings and thoughts as you resist making corrections or as you look at the 'mistake.'

    _____

    _____

    _____

    _____

4. How do you 'check' yourself during the day? Notice times when you are looking into mirrors, adjusting clothing or hair and picking on or detailing yourself, others or your surroundings. What are your thoughts and feelings during these moments?

_____

_____

_____

_____

5. Recall times when you have let go of the need for perfection or control. What fears did you have to overcome while doing this? What was the outcome of the situation when you did let go?

_____

_____

_____

_____

Journeying Through Life

Philosopher Friedrich Nietzsche put forth a wonderful scenario: "What if a demon were to creep after you one night, in your loneliest loneliness, and say, 'This life which you live must be lived by you once again and innumerable times more; and every pain and joy and thought and sigh must come again to you, all in the same sequence. The eternal hourglass will again and again be turned and you with it, dust of the dust!' Would you throw yourself down and gnash your teeth and curse that demon? Or would you answer, 'Never have I heard anything more divine.'"

How would you answer the nocturnal demon? Simple put, are you living a life you would want to live again—one rich with meaning, connection and joy?

Similarly, we may ponder being on our deathbed and wonder if we would have any regrets. This reality check, especially as we enter midlife, calls for some existential reflection. A content place to be when our physical time on Earth is done is not to want to cry because our life is over but to celebrate because we lived; yet, how many people do you know who could face death with true satisfaction?

As writer Christopher Morley stated, "there is only one success—to be able to spend your life in your own way." Likewise, Carl Jung suggested that "the sole purpose of human existence is to kindle a light in the darkness of mere being." We want to move through our lives with meaning, insight, and integrity—to 'step up to the plate' and face courageously whatever we have been summoned to be.

We want to live our lives in such a way that when our feet hit the floor in the morning, Satan shudders and says, "Oh shit! You're awake!" In most cases, our fearful egos sadly bench us before we have eaten breakfast. Thoughts of 'what if' and 'I'd really like to' are swept away by our habitual coping mechanisms and internal, negating voices.

Philosopher St. Augustine noticed our reluctance to question what is happening as we journey through life. He stated that "people travel to wonder at the height of mountains, at the huge waves of the sea, at the long courses of rivers, at the vast compass of the ocean, at the circular motion of the stars; and they pass by themselves without wondering."

It is the aware, insightful and curious who ponder their lives and how they choose to live them. They courageously turn inward, looking humbly and honestly at patterns of behaviour in order to take ownership of their feelings and responses and find ways to live in a more consciously and humanely. Others choose not to look or to ask, afraid to face what they might find if they did begin to look. Perhaps they once began, and their weakened egos sadly turned in fright.

Ultimately, we have choices and are solely responsible for our lives. In her poem, 'When Death Comes,' Mary Oliver reflects, "When it is over, I don't want to wonder/ if I have made of my life something particular, and real./ I don't want to find myself sighing and frightened,/ or full of argument./ I don't want to end up simply having visited this world." Similarly, sportswriter Grantland Rice stated, "When the One Great Scorer comes to write against your name, He marks—not that you won or lost—but how you played the game."

<u>Reflections</u>

1. How would you answer Nietzsche's demon? What parts of your life would you avoid reliving and why?

    _____

    _____

    _____

    _____

2. Imagine you were told you only had a short time left to live. What regrets surface? What could you do to lessen any of these regrets? How do you approach your impending death?

    _____

    _____

    _____

    _____

3. What questions do you avoid asking yourself, perhaps already knowing the answer? Deep down, what is psyche asking you to do or to 'step up to' that you are not addressing?

    _____

    _____

    _____

    _____

4. In what way and in what situations do you feel you are merely 'visiting' this world? Identify the distractions, addictions and other coping mechanism that prevent you from living a 'particular' life.

_____

_____

_____

_____

5. Reflect upon Jung's statement: "The sole purpose of human existence is to kindle a light in the darkness of mere being." What does this mean for you and how you choose to live your life?

_____

_____

_____

_____

Finding Your Own Path

You may be familiar with author Henry David Thoreau's saying, "If a man does not keep pace with his companions, perhaps it is because he hears a different drummer. Let him step to the music which he hears, however measured or far away." Thoreau metaphorically advises 'be yourself,' but what does it mean to step to one's own music?

Psychologist Abraham Maslow used the term *self-actualization* to describe the final level of psychological development. At this stage, the full personal potential of the individual is realized. Carl Jung offered the concept of individuation as a psychological process that makes one truly a unique, genuine and passionate being.

Jungian author Murray Stein explained individuation as "the inner union of pieces of the psyche that were divided and split off by earlier developmental demands and processes." "Demands and processes" refers to childhood wounding in which authentic parts of ourselves were repressed into the unconscious. During individuation, our outward personas, who we think we are, are introduced to our repressed shadow material. The task is to meet, take ownership and reintegrate these 'bad' or undervalued parts into our beings and apply them in our outer world.

Individuation involves separating ourselves from conformity and from the collective. Thoreau stated, "Let everyone mind his own business, and endeavor to be what he was made." Indeed, individuation promotes choosing from an internal reference point rather than relying upon the collective norms of what we 'should,' 'have to' or 'must' do. As we detach from mother, father, family and society, a loss of dependency results in personal suffering.

Jung suggested that one "must offer a ransom in place of himself, that is, he must bring forth values which are an equivalent substitute for his absence in the collective personal sphere." The painful price is feeling and accepting that we are truly alone. The reward is moving towards living a life larger than our egos and the collective norms. We end up living a life more aligned with who we truly are. As the Chinese philosopher Lao Tzu stated, "when I let go of what I am, I become what I might be."

Becoming who we truly are meant to be is living according to our true potential. Jung pondered, "What is it, in the end, that induces a man to go his own way and to rise out of unconscious identity with the mass as out of a swathing mist?" His answer was 'vocation': "an irrational factor that destines a man to emancipate himself from the herd and from its well-worn paths." As writer Ralph Waldo Emerson advised, "do not go where the path may lead; go instead where there is no path and leave a trail."

Often people think individuation is self-absorbing, ego gratifying and selfish. To the contrary, it is about becoming a mature adult, responsible for our actions. As we break free from family and societal beliefs that once bound us, we are able to offer to others and community our genuine selves. As Jung stated, "individuation does not shut one out from the world, but gathers the world to itself."

Reflections

1.   What are the 'shoulds,' 'have to's,' and 'musts' that have influenced and continue to influence your life?

   _____

   _____

   _____

   _____

2.   What are the parts of yourself—the traits, labels and roles—that prevent you from stepping off your existing path onto a new, more soulful path?

   _____

   _____

   _____

   _____

3.   What qualities of yourself do you know deep down that you could offer to self, family and community? How do you feel when you think about what you could give?

   _____

   _____

   _____

   _____

4.   Society and family have a huge influence in how we live our lives. How might the family, peers and community you live among react to any change or path redirection you are contemplating?

   _____

   _____

   _____

   _____

5. What fears surface as you contemplate increased awareness and honouring of your true desires and living more aligned to your true self?

_____

_____

_____

_____

What Are You Being Called to Serve?

In *Tuesdays with Morrie*, by Mitch Albom, Morrie Schwartz, stated, "So many people walk around with a meaningless life. They seem half-asleep, even when they're busy doing things they think are important. This is because they're chasing the wrong things. The way you get meaning into your life is to devote yourself to loving others, devote yourself to your community around you, and devote yourself to creating something that gives you purpose and meaning." Where and how does one find this purpose and meaning?

Recall that individuation is the process of becoming who you are meant to be. One task of individuation is to serve what your deepest self asks you to be—often referred to as *vocation*. Carl Jung defined vocation as "an irrational factor that destines a man to emancipate himself from the herd and from its well-worn paths." He further explained that "true personality is always a vocation . . . from which there is no escape." Vocation must be obeyed "as if it were a daemon whispering to [you] of new and wonderful paths." The whisper is your calling.

James Hollis asked, "Where is the unlived life which haunts, or summons, or intimates you?" We are all "called to spiritual greatness"—to be who we truly are, regardless of the costs. We are all summoned to the challenge to live this life.

Even for a fleeting moment, we deeply know that something else could better feed our souls, but we generally do not serve this calling. Our frightened egos, content with the security of how it has always been, avoid, have little regard for and shut down the inner calling, deadening our souls.

Rumi made this tragic analogy: "A king sent you to a country to carry out one special, specific task. You go to the country and you perform a hundred other tasks, but if you have not performed the task you were sent for, it is as if you have performed nothing at all."

Often it is difficult to recognize our calling, as we may think a summons is coming from our true selves when, indeed, it may be coming from our egos. How do we know the difference? The discernment will involve making a choice between how we have been living or believing and a new way. Choosing a new way involves personal conflict and the requirement of detachment from our normal ways of being, resulting in some suffering and personal growth.

When we best serve ourselves, we can best serve others and humanity. A calling feels, as Hollis suggested, as if "something is in fact choosing us." The choice to accept and follow the vocation often requires us to leave a comfortable and familiar stance and move into the unknown, guided by a deeper force.

In the film, *Miss Potter*, Beatrix Potter's father asked her, "Why do you find it necessary to leave your home?" She replied, "It is not a choice. There's nothing else I can do."

Vocation brings the purpose and meaning Schwartz referred to. When we follow our calling, we feel an inner sense of rightness and well-being. We are fulfilling our highest duty—not a duty to family, society or to ego, but to our true selves. We feel contentment, deep satisfaction and joy.

Reflections

1. When we are following our vocations or true selves, it feels like we are 'on-the-right track' and situations flow. Recall times in which you felt this way. Recall times when you seemed to be chosen and soulfully felt as if a situation was choosing you. What did you have to leave behind in order to follow this feeling?

    _____

    _____

    _____

    _____

2. What do you think you have been summoned to be? Remember, vocation is not a job or role but rather a way of purposely being in the world, living in deep accordance with who you truly are. What soul whispers fleetingly call you and yet are negated?

    _____

    _____

    _____

3. Name the 'hundred other tasks' that you do which divert you from following your vocation. What might you be doing instead of these activities?

    _____

    _____

    _____

    _____

4. Recall a time when you were drawn to something that you thought at the time was a vocation but was actually ego-driven. What feelings did you experience and what needs were being fulfilled? Often, ego-driven desires bring high levels of excitement and expectations for life becoming 'better.' Vocation is grounded in rightness and satisfies your soul.

_____

_____

_____

_____

5. Vocation serves self and humanity. What gifts do you have that not only bring you alive but also enhance the lives of others? How can you bring these attributes into your daily life?

_____

_____

_____

_____

Finding Bliss

You may see bumper stickers that advise you to "Follow your bliss" and read travel, spa and even restaurant advertisements that promise blissful experiences. What exactly is bliss?

The term *bliss* comes from an English word originally meaning "outward lightheartedness, merriment, happiness and joy." It is related to the Sanskrit word, *ananda,* which roughly translates as "supreme happiness or ecstasy." From a psychologically perspective, bliss moves you from the external to an internal feeling of being in soulful or spiritual harmony or peace with not only yourself but with the entire Universe.

Before you can follow your bliss, you must find it. Decades of not following your bliss make it difficult to know exactly what your bliss is. However, you get moments of bliss when you are living according to your true self. Those 'aha' moments, the spontaneous tears, the unplanned laughter, and partaking in passionate interests that are deeply meaningful indicate bliss. These times are when your soul lets you know, "I'm here with you and I like it."

To find your bliss, start by doing more of what truly gives you feelings of inner joy, peace and contentment. Take an honest look at how your thinking and actions affect you. Think the thoughts and hold the possibilities that bring a heartfelt smile to you. Start to let go of beliefs, expectations and roles that restrict who you truly are. Notice when the 'can'ts,' 'shoulds' and 'are you crazy' thoughts arise. What part of you does not want you to follow your bliss? What would following your bliss mean for you and for others?

When you begin to follow your bliss, ideas, situations and opportunities begin to flow. As mythology scholar Joseph Campbell, who coined the phrase, 'follow your bliss,' advised, "find where it is, and don't be afraid to follow it . . . . Doors will open where you would not have thought there would be doors." As you begin to trust your inner wisdom more, you begin to get glimpses of possibilities and of hopes for a better way of living your life.

Bliss is not found by looking outwardly—you find bliss within. Although you were born with bliss, it was buried or put aside as you chose paths that served others more than served yourself. Campbell stated, "If you follow your bliss, you put yourself on a kind of track that has been there all the while, waiting for you, and the life that you ought to be living is the one you are living." Carl Jung called the search for your path in life individuation. He emphasized the need to reach an understanding of your own individuality and purpose and to embrace your "innermost, last, and incomparable uniqueness." Finding your passionate path evokes a capacity for self-love and love of others, for healing, and for the feeling that your life has meaning. Meaning brings bliss.

According to Campbell, bliss occurs when "our life experiences on the purely physical plane will have resonances with our own innermost being and reality, so that we actually feel the rapture of being alive." Ah, the rapture of being alive! This is bliss—a feeling that you are living a life aligned with your true self—the life you were intended to live. Spiritual leader Howard Thurman further suggested, "Go out and do what makes you come alive, because what the world needs most are people who have come alive."

Reflections

1. What 'makes you come alive?' Where have you found moments of bliss? Name the track that has your name on it.

    _____

    _____

    _____

    _____

2. What prevents you from doing more of what brings you bliss? Identify fears and self-limitations that surface when contemplating blissful experiences.

    _____

    _____

    _____

    _____

3. When in your life have you experienced flow? Recall the mindset and shift in attitudes that accompanied the flow.

    _____

    _____

    _____

    _____

4. What causes you to come off the bliss track or lose flow? How do other peoples' reactions or feedback to your bliss affect you?

    _____

    _____

    _____

    _____

5. Incorporate blissful activities or even blissful thoughts into your daily life. Try doing this for three weeks and take note of the results.

_____

_____

_____

_____

The Importance of Feelings

"Sit there and smile" and "Never contradict your father" are statements we may have been told in the name of good manners. We learned very early what was acceptable in family and social settings. We sat up straight, suppressed our tears and laughter, and consciously decided, "I better not say that."

Carl Jung stated that "repression is a process that begins in early childhood under the moral influence of the environment and continues through life." For the most part, we learned to repress qualities and feelings that were uncomfortable for our primary caregivers. These childhood lessons met and continue to meet other people's needs; however, they did not and currently do not have our souls in mind.

A common childhood lesson is 'to be nice.' A closer look reveals that 'nice' involves acting pleasant, being overly cooperative, and 'biting our tongue.' We respond with, "Whatever you want." In fact, being 'nice' is being more concerned about what others think and feel than what you think and feel. When we are nice, we most likely suppress our thoughts, feelings, intuition and wants.

For the most part, we live in an emotionally illiterate society and are not practiced in expressing and receiving feelings. We feel embarrassed or vulnerable when talking about certain feelings. We silence ourselves so we might not hurt someone with our truths. Ironically, we end up hurting our bodies and souls when we withhold what we feel and want.

Emotions exist to let us know that this choice or situation does or does not match what is right for us. Feelings connect with our ability to notice and trust our gut reactions. When we do not fully feel, we become detached from our intuition and deciding what is best for us. We may begin to question our ability to make soulful decisions.

When we do not express feelings and wants, we rely upon a range of passive and aggressive responses. Examples of these behaviours include gossiping, sarcasm, blaming, anger, the silent treatment, lying and compliance. These actions avoid dealing with real feelings and often lead to more intense feelings of anger, depression and resentment.

Our bodies become diseased when stressful feelings are not expressed. The highly controlled Type-A personality's ability to suppress hostility has been linked to increased cholesterol and blood pressure and heart attacks. Cancer specialist Dr. W. Douglas Brodie has identified a Type-C or cancer personality that is characterized by the suppression of anger and resentment and by a strong tendency to be a nice, non-assertive people-pleaser.

Another way to look at withholding feelings is seeing it as not being fully present with others and with yourself but only showing up with your body and mind. A great place to start is merely expressing the emotion by stating, "I feel disappointed." Rather than covering up feelings by saying, "Oh, don't be mad," validate other people's feelings by using reflective statements such as, "You sound angry."

Most of us find that when we take a risk and practice emotional honesty, we feel closer to others. We soon realize that others have feelings, too, and like us, need to be heard without being judged, criticized, fixed or having to defend ourselves.

Reflections

1. Recall how you saw your parents, especially the same-sex parent, express their feelings and opinions. What did you learn about how men and women handle feelings?

    _____

    _____

    _____

    _____

2. What does 'being nice' or being a nice person mean to you? How was 'being nice' valued in your family of origin? How much does this initial learning affect how you currently relate with others?

    _____

    _____

    _____

    _____

3. Reflect upon times as a child when you expressed different emotions. What were the consequences of each expression? When you were persistent, for example, you may have been called 'stubborn' by your mother. When you felt pride in yourself, perhaps you were told, "You shouldn't let your head get too big." What did you actually learn from these responses?

    _____

    _____

    _____

    _____

4. Look for times when you use passive responses such as the silent treatment, sighing, avoidance of conflict, rolling your eyes, over-smiling and whining. Similarly, watch for assertive behaviour such as sarcasm, slamming objects, using threats, blaming, using 'you' statements and yelling. Later, think of an alternative assertive way of handling the situation using feelings and wants.

_____

_____

_____

_____

5. Become acquainted with the range of feelings by referring to a feelings list. One possible source is The Centre for Nonviolent Communication's 'Feelings Inventory' found at: http://www.cnvc.org/Training/feelings-inventory

_____

_____

_____

_____

Learning to Be More Assertive

"Excuse me, my soup is cold. I would like it heated up." For many, stating this to a server in a calm, respectful manner is difficult. Why is it so difficult to ask for what we want?

Many people were raised in homes in which their thoughts and emotions were not valued. We learned that our inner world of feelings and desires was not worthy, and certainly could not be voiced safely. As a result, we became detached from our true wants and feelings, resulting in living lives that only partial fulfill us and slowly erode our souls.

Expressing what you are feeling and asking for what you want is called *assertiveness*. Being assertive equalizes relationships, decreases feelings of victimization, and lessens any resentment for not saying or doing what you truly want to do or say. Being assertive not only increases your ability to communicate but also promotes respect for yourself and from others.

Believing you have a right to voice interests, feelings and ideas the same as everyone else does is key to being assertive, but you may feel guilty in stating what you want. Stating your ideas does not mean you are selfish, rude or unreasonable. Although what you say may not please or may differ from others, realize that sometimes what you want for yourself is not what others want for you or, more importantly, for themselves.

Indeed, as you become more conscious and break away from your habitual ways of being nice, others may not be comfortable with this shift. Remember, being nice is about looking after the needs of others before your needs. People will notice, be curious and even feel angry that their needs are not being attended to at the same previous level. If stating your wants and feelings is uncomfortable for others, this may be an opportunity for them to self-reflect or for an honest discussion about what they were expecting from you.

Assertively saying 'no' can also be challenging for people. It is helpful to remember that when someone asks us something, there are two possible answers, 'yes' or 'no," and perhaps a third, "I'll let you know later." As we become more confident in knowing and asking for what we want, we become comfortable with others saying 'no' to us. Similarly, disagreements we receive will no longer be felt as personal criticism because we understand that other people are merely stating opinions and wants, just as we can and do.

As much as assertiveness appears easy for some, decades of being passive makes attempting change awkward. Begin to develop awareness of body sensations, feelings and intuition. Listen for inner beliefs that counter your assertiveness, such as, "You don't have the right to say no" or "How dare you say that." Reflect upon the source of these thoughts and any accompanying feelings such as guilt, fear or shame.

Become comfortable using phrases such as "I would like . . . ," "I prefer . . . ," and, "No thanks." Practice in situations that are emotionally safe such as with a close friend. As the pendulum shifts away from passiveness, we experience a more fulfilling and soulful way of being. As the author Shakti Gawain stated, "assertiveness is not what you do, it's who you are."

Reflections

1. How would certain people react if you increased your assertiveness? Might this possible reaction be hindering your assertiveness? Take a closer look at the needs that are currently being fulfilled by you and others. How would the needs of all parties shift as you became more assertive?

   _____

   _____

   _____

   _____

2. Do you have friends/acquaintances you do not actually enjoy or have much in common with but feel obligated to continue seeing? These obligations may also exist with family situations. Ask yourself, "Why am I continuing to partake in these activities?" and "What is the cost to my soul of maintaining these relationships?"

   _____

   _____

   _____

   _____

3. Are there times when you avoid saying what you truly feel or stating your opinions because it may make someone upset or the person may not agree with you? Focus on the specific situations or people that affect you this way. What underlying fears may be preventing you from stating what you genuinely feel or think?

   _____

   _____

   _____

   _____

4. Do you feel criticized or bad when someone disagrees or is upset, disappointed or angry with you? What were you needing or expecting from that person that their reaction did not provide? Think of ways you can fulfill this need without relying on others.

    _____

    _____

    _____

    _____

5. Do you ever feel that some person or situation is 'taking advantage of' you? Remember, unless we are truly threatened, no one ever 'makes us' do anything. In these moments, try to identify what part of you is taking advantage of yourself. What are you 'making' yourself do that you would rather not do?

    _____

    _____

    _____

    _____

How Do You Handle Anger?

Buddha suggested that "holding on to anger is like grasping a hot coal with the intent of throwing it at someone else; you are the one who gets burned." This is a perfect image of the way people often handle anger.

As infants, we cried and even screamed as a way of releasing our distressing emotions and discomfort. For the most part, our cries were 'what babies do' and evoked others to get us food, change our diapers and hold us. As we learned to use our words, parents and society discouraged us from crying or showing other forms of dissatisfaction, especially in public.

We were taught to repress anger and to deny or rationalize any issue regarding it. We learned there was 'no sense in fighting' and began to shut down any voicing of displeasure. In Latin, *angere* means "to throttle and torment." The word *anger* originates from the word *angus*, meaning "narrow, painfully constricted" and "a strangling." Indeed, unexpressed anger often shows up in throat-related symptoms such as a sore throat or laryngitis.

Anger not expressed authentically is mismanaged anger and shows up in different anger styles. People who somatize suppress their anger due to fear of rejection or disapproval. They become passive, often playing the role of martyr. Anger in this case shows up in the body as migraines, ulcers, colitis, arthritis, TMJ, breast cancer and coronary heart problems. Conversely, those who explode verbally and/or physically express anger that has been held in and is released aggressively onto people and creatures not even involved with the initial anger. This anger style shows up as road rage and animal abuse.

Self-punishers passively channel their anger into guilt and punish themselves. This form of anger shows up in behaviours such as excessive crying, drinking, eating, shopping and even cutting themselves. Some people underhandedly express their anger in aggressive ways that are deemed more socially acceptable. In this case, anger shows up as revenge, sabotage, sarcasm, complaining, blaming and gossiping and is a means to control others.

We all mismanage anger sometimes and tend to use some anger styles more often than other ones. How can we express our anger better? First, know your anger style so you can become aware of it sooner in order to stop your behaviour. Then, address your true feelings. Start with, "I am angry!" Like any strong reaction, view anger as a tool for inner reflection and growth.

Take ownership of your anger and ask, "What am I really angry about?" In many cases, the source of the anger is something you did or did not do. In other cases, it may be long repressed childhood anger that continues to interfere with current happenings.

For the most part, anger occurs to tell us something needs to change. We often feel angry when injustice or something unfair has happened to us and/or to others. The frustration or anger may propel us to take action such as make a phone call, write a letter, or finally sign up for a long-desired, yet negated, course or social action group. In this way, anger has been sublimated into constructive action. As you consciously observe your red-hot anger, you cool its volatility, and are able to hold it and use its warmth as a catalyst for creative change.

Reflections

1.   Identify your styles of handling anger. Under what circumstances do you tend to use each one? Why is each style used with different people or situations?

_____

_____

_____

_____

2.   How was anger expressed (or not) in your family of origin? What were the consequences of expressing anger in your household? Recall the times you expressed anger. What did you learn about anger during these situations?

_____

_____

_____

_____

3.   Anger is often the tip of the iceberg, with feelings of sadness, embarrassment, resentment, jealousy and loss underlying. Think of a time in which you were angry. What were the primary emotions beneath the surface of the anger?

_____

_____

_____

_____

4. How does anger show up in your body? Identify different body sensations that manifest as anger begins and escalates. Examples may include placing hands on the hips, clenched fists, increased heartbeat, shifting the jaw or flushing.

_____

_____

_____

_____

5. Recognize the times you feel like swearing or do swear. Remember, to swear is to take an oath, to assert or to uphold the truth, and to state your truth. What are you standing up for?

_____

_____

_____

_____

What Do You Really Need?

"I need a vacation!" "I really need a new pair of shoes." The term *need* refers to "necessity, compulsion and duty" and may have been influenced by the Old English word *neod* meaning "desire and longing." What do we truly need?

Wants, such as the vacation and shoes, are not essential to survival, but they can improve our quality of life. Desires are extremely urgent wants. Needs, on the other hand, are essential for survival. Beyond the obvious physical needs for survival, such as food, water and shelter, we require the fulfilment of psychological needs. As children, this fulfilment falls onto the responsibility of parents or primary caregivers. These needs, called ego needs, helped us achieve and maintain confidence and self-esteem.

One ego need is for *mirroring* and is a need to feel affirmed, recognized and accepted especially when able to show ourselves. We experienced this when parents acknowledged and appreciated an accomplished or attempted task or a specific quality in us. The *idealizing* need is a need for acceptance by a calm, wise and protective situation or person that possesses the qualities we lack. This occurred when we looked up to a teacher or parent and they reflected care and respect back to us rather than showing authority or power.

The need for *twinship* is the need to experience an essential likeness with a desired person or situation. Examples may have been feeling part of the family, a club or a culture. This fostered in us a sense of support and belonging. The *adversarial* need is a need to experience a caring, opposing force that continues to be supportive and responsive while allowing or even encouraging us to be in active opposition. This may have occurred when we were given permission to have different opinions than our parents, debate ideas and still feel loved regardless of these differences.

Efficacy is needed in order to feel that we have an impact and are able to evoke what we need. A simple example is that we learned that (hopefully) a parent or caregiver would come to feed us, change our diapers or hold us when we cried. We learned that we have the ability to initiate, to ask for and to achieve fulfillment of needs on our own, forming a sense of self-empowerment.

Once these basic psychological needs have been met and as we reached adolescence, the task for us was to become less dependent on external sources for the gratification of our needs. Ideally, if our needs were fulfilled, we now have our own inner resources and enough self-esteem so as not to rely so heavily upon others to fulfill them.

It is important to realize that needs are meet intraphysically—not through the interpersonal relationship between you and others who are involved in any experience, but rather through the experience itself that provokes a self-sustaining feeling of your selfhood.

Unfortunately, for the most part, parents do not do a complete job of meeting our needs. The consequence of unfilled childhood needs is the often unconscious search for the fulfillment of these needs in our adult relationships whether it is with friends, spouses, co-workers or with our children. We continue to look externally, as we did as children, to have our needs met; however, as adults, we need to look inwardly to fulfill our needs.

Reflections

1. Take each of the five needs and reflect upon how and to what degree each was meet in your childhood. This may evoke some very poignant realizations. Keep in mind that all parents are incapable of fulfilling all our needs.

    _____

    _____

    _____

    _____

2. How do you tend to get the five needs met now? You may want to reflect upon how your need fulfillment activities have changed over the decades. Usually, they tend to move from external to internal sources.

    _____

    _____

    _____

    _____

3. Reflect on the neediness that may still exist between you and your parents. What needs are you still hoping they will fulfill? What needs might your parents be expecting you to fulfill? If you feel the hurtful zings, you may still be experiencing disappointment in regard to needs that your parents are incapable of fulfilling.

    _____

    _____

    _____

    _____

4. What does your soul 'need'? What does your ego want?

_____

_____

_____

_____

5. Reflect upon the concept that 'needs are met intraphysically.'

_____

_____

_____

_____

Fulfilling Your Needs

How do you know whether your needs are being fulfilled at any moment? Begin by looking at your feelings as they tell you if needs are being satisfied or are lacking. Ask yourself, "How am I feeling?" while or immediately after doing a certain activity (e.g., watching TV, doing a task, or being with a certain person).

A simple way to monitor how you are feeling is to look at your energy level. Is this a thumb-up or a thumb-down situation? Thumbs-down feelings (e.g., sad, anxious, frustrated) indicate needs are not being satisfied. Thumbs-up feelings (e.g., joyful, relaxed) indicate that the situation is meeting your needs. In each situation, try to identify what exactly is draining or filling your needs cup. Be aware of any expectations you may have placed onto the situation or person. The low energy may be due to your unmet expectations around certain needs being satisfied by others and not on the actual situation.

In seeking to meet your needs, you have to be careful not to be tricked into meeting them in unhealthy ways such as addictions, risky or obsessive behaviour, or any other undesirable activity. Although these actions temporarily meet your needs, they are not in the long or even short term best for your soul. The effect of the drug, activity, or contact with another person ceases and you literally come down from your psychological high, often feeling worse. You want to be able to fulfill needs and make choices with some degree of consciousness.

Think of instances when an inner voice has said, "I need . . . ." You could finish this sentence with 'more chocolate,' 'another drink,' 'to go shopping' or 'to call my ex-partner.' The key is to identify how were you feeling or what you were thinking just before the need statement popped into consciousness. Most often you were feeling uncomfortable feelings associated with negative self-talk (e.g., 'I'm no good' or 'I feel lonely.'). Recall the types of needs described in the previous chapter. Identify which needs were not being fulfilled at that moment. Name an action or thought you might do instead which would fulfill that need. This alternative might be going for a walk or saying an affirmation to yourself such as, "I am loved."

Unhealthy need fulfillment often appears in relationships. Both partners unconsciously fall into dysfunctional roles such as Caregiver, Rescuer or Wounded Child. You may feel comfortable in these roles, but you are really acting out childhood roles, unconsciously hoping to get your unfilled needs met. You may temporarily get your needs met, but more often than not, you will become disappointed by, even resentful of, the other person. If insightful enough, you realize you are actually resentful of yourself for once again trying to obtain something you cannot get from someone else.

James Hollis advised asking yourself, "What am I asking others to do for me that, as a mature adult, I need to be doing for myself?" Additionally, you can reflect upon Hollis' question, "Am I taking too much responsibility for the emotional well-being of others?" If so, why? These are tough but essential questions to ask.

Carl Jung believed that our unfulfilled needs and missing qualities are met not by searching outwardly or with others but are found within. Even if we are in a positive relationship, we are ultimately alone and required to take responsibility for our feelings and needs.

Reflections

1. From the previous chapter's reflections, consider the ways you get your needs met. Identify which ways are considered healthy and which are unhealthy. How might you alter the unhealthy ones?

    _____

    _____

    _____

    _____

2. When the thought of, 'I need a _____' arises, identify the feelings (usually uncomfortable) that accompanying the situation. How do your feelings in the specific situation relate to any childhood experiences of unmet needs?

    _____

    _____

    _____

    _____

3. James Hollis stated that as adults, we need to "take personal responsibility for our lives" and must "maturely acknowledge" that our parents and our partners have not and will not ever rescue us. To what degree do you live by this statement? In what situations might a part of you still be hoping for or expecting needs to be fulfilled by others?

    _____

    _____

    _____

    _____

4. Recall times when you left a person or event and felt
    low or disappointed. Try to discern whether your ego
    expectations were not being met or the situation truly
    did not meet your needs.

    _____

    _____

    _____

    _____

5. Hollis further suggested that "when you take care of
    yourself, fulfill your own needs, you relieve your partner,
    family or friends of this impossible task, freeing them
    and yourself of dysfunctional roles and expectations."
    Where in the past have you let go of expecting others
    to fulfill your needs? What shift in your way of thinking
    had to occur? What were the results for everyone
    involved?

    _____

    _____

    _____

    _____

The Parental Imago
in Our Relationships

"Repetition compulsion" is the term Sigmund Freud assigned to the phenomenon in which we repeat a traumatic event or put ourselves in situations where a certain event is likely to happen again. These occurrences suggest that we are seemingly unconsciously compelled to reexperience distressing situations. Noticeably, this suffering often appears in relationships where we exclaim, "Why does this keep happening to me?"

Our earliest relational experiences, usual parent-child ones, form the template and program our images of how we are to act within relationships. Our childhood psyches form parental imagos, based on both direct experience with our actual parents and from archetypal or collective elements of the ideal caretaker. Carl Jung termed this over-valued, emotionally laden and deified view of mother and father the *parental imago*. He later named it the parental *archetype* or the parental *complex*.

Our parents, for the most part, accepted this idealized image. The task of our parents was to reflect back and restore in us this idealized image through the fulfillment of our needs. In this way, we develop self-esteem, learn self-governance and self-advocacy and, most importantly, learn the efficacy of meeting our needs. The imago or projection is removed from the parents. If, however, needs were not fully met, the parental imago remains energized within our psyches. We will continue to carry and project this idealized image onto others in hopes of fulfilling our unmet childhood needs.

When we are triggered unconsciously—for example, when we fall in love—the parental imago is reanimated. We regress, returning to childhood relationship behaviour. James Hollis suggested "that the original attraction to the partner was in great part guided by the parental imago. That unconscious image is projected onto potential partners until someone comes along who can catch it and hold it." Similarly, we will catch and hold onto the images our potential partners place on us.

The roles, expectations and familiar scripts that were imprinted into our psyches along with the parental imagos compel us to repeat maladaptive patterns of relating with others. As adults, we often choose contrary to this template. This over-compensation is an unconscious act, as we are still trapped or reacting to our early parental imagos. There has been no conscious discernment of how we want to act; and we are merely doing the opposite. When we proclaim, "I'll never be like my dad!" we are still using the original 'dad' imago as a reference point. In all cases, the key motivator is the fulfillment of our unmet childhood needs and our partners' needs.

We often think that once we are out of the relationship or once our parents are deceased, everything will be all right. Unfortunately, we still have the parental imago regardless of the geographically proximity or living status of our parents. As writer William Faulkner succinctly stated, "the past is not dead, it is not even past."

Until childhood wounds from flawed or 'not good enough' parenting are acknowledged and until you stop projecting your parental imagos, you, as Jung noted, are bound to be "a slave of what you need in your soul." Jung advised, "So long as a positive or negative resemblance to the parents is the deciding factor in a love choice, the release from the parental imago, and hence from childhood, is not complete."

Reflections

1. What patterns do you see in friend and partner relationships? What "keeps happening" to you in your relationships?

_____

_____

_____

_____

2. What idealized or negative imago did you have of your parents as a child? What are your current parental imagos?

_____

_____

_____

_____

3. How do you behave in intimate partner relationships? Note your regressions and any child-parent dynamics. How does your behaviour change when in the presence of your partner or potential partner?

_____

_____

_____

_____

4. What unmet childhood needs are you still hoping to fulfill? If you could hear just one statement from a parent, what would that be? What is the ultimate feeling that you want to have when with a partner (e.g., special, loved, smart)?

_____

_____

_____

_____

5. Where does Faulkner's comment, "The past is not dead, it is not even past," hold true in your life?

_____

_____

_____

_____

Leaving the Childhood Home

In the movie, *Miss Potter*, Beatrix, who has decided to move out on her own, is asked by her father, "Why do you find it necessary to leave your home?" She replied, "It is not a choice . . . . I must make my own way." Indeed, we all must eventually leave not only our physical but also our psychic childhood homes.

Parents play a key role in their children's psychological development. Most parents, like most adults, do not take responsibility for their unconscious material, be it moods, projections or coping mechanisms. As Carl Jung suggested, these unhealthy attitudes "radiate out into the environment and, if there are children, infect them too." How exactly have we been 'infected'?

As children, we may have received love only based upon our fulfillment of certain roles or behaviours. We adapted and became 'good girls and boys,' acted how we were 'supposed to' and gave up parts of ourselves which were undervalued, perhaps even envied, by our parents.

As children, we may have been confused by chaotic and conflicting parental messages. We were not encouraged to express our feelings and opinions. We were required to live a life based more upon the needs of our parents than our own. Oppressive parental influence shows up in parents trying to live what they did not achieve through our academic, social and athletic accomplishments.

Our parents' actions resulted in psychic wounding. Their seemingly innocuous actions obstructed us from growing into who we were truly meant to be. Unconscious parental attitudes have been introjected and internalized into our psyches, where they became inner, dominating voices that currently seem to originate from us.

Jung stated, "Nothing has a stronger influence psychologically on . . . children than the unlived life of the parent." Jung believed that parents' unlived life is "that part of their lives which might have been lived had not certain somewhat threadbare excuses prevented the parents from doing so. To put it bluntly, it is that part of life which they have always shirked." Instead of maturely accepting their past losses and possible regrets, our parents' hopes were transferred to us.

We are also affected indirectly through the attitudes we instinctively take towards our parents' states of mind: either we fight against them with spoken (if safe) and unspoken protest or else we succumb to a paralyzing and habitual imitation. In both cases, we are obliged to do, to feel and to live not in reaction to what we want but as our parents want. As children, and now as adults, we need to claim our own psychic self-sovereignty.

Parents are not asked to be perfect, but rather, they should make sincere efforts to acknowledge their weak points and unconscious material. According to Jung, parents "should at least come to terms with them consciously; they should make it a duty to work out their inner difficulties for the sake of the children."

When unconscious material is addressed responsibly by parents, children are relieved of a burden that ultimately was not theirs to begin with. Parents can genuinely encourage their children to step into their own authentic selves full of acceptance, self-esteem and autonomy.

Reflections

1. As a child, how did you 'adapt' to your parents' needs?
    What behaviour or traits did you have to suppress or
    overplay in order to be accepted or to fit into the family
    dynamic? What did you provide for your parents?

    _____

    _____

    _____

    _____

2. Can you identify the unlived lives of your parents?
    What did they often dream about that never occurred
    for them?

    _____

    _____

    _____

    _____

3. Identify your introjected voices or messages that
    originated with your parents. Rewrite or reframe these
    messages into a positive statement about yourself.

    _____

    _____

    _____

    _____

4. How have your attitudes been influenced by your parents' states of mind? Identify where your attitudes tend to rebel or protest against them and where you habitually succumb to them. Honestly explore if your attitudes are truly how you feel now.

    _____

    _____

    _____

    _____

5. If you are a parent, look at how your unconscious material has and continues to influence your children. Begin to remove these expectations and hopes from your children and observe any shifts that may occur.

    _____

    _____

    _____

    _____

We Are Complex in More Ways Than One

In many myths, a dark destructive force, whether Zeus or the Devil, often appears in an ambush, thwarting the hero's best intentions. This negating and often judging, critical and disdainful force causes chaos and disorientation, often stunning the hero into a dispirited psychic place. Psychologically, this destructive force is called a *complex*.

Complexes are deeply rooted in us and can be traced back to our childhoods. They are a collection of associations, ideas, opinions and beliefs that are grouped around sensitive feelings. Apple pie, cottage vacations, ballet and the smell of hair dye may be bundled together with the feeling of not being good enough forming a Mother complex. Conversely, a Father complex may be composed of a certain style of hat, the smell of Jack Daniels, Sunday afternoon football games and the feeling of unconditional acceptance.

The activation of a complex is always marked by the presence of some strong emotion, be it love, hate, anger, anxiety or sadness. When our buttons are pushed, a complex has been activated. Tears begin to swell. We 'fly off the handle' for no apparent reason. When activated, we speak, act and feel out of the complex, not how we would want to. We later think, 'What was that all about?'

Complex energy is separate from our usual personality, and thus, we are usually unconscious of it; however, it appears when triggered from outer associations. Certain topics or situations have a personal charge to them. A simple example of a complex at work is when someone becomes agitated or angry when hearing another person talk about his or her mother. Someone else may become overly activated when seeing a person victimized.

Complexes can also be formed when we overly identify with specific roles and tasks, creating an elevated amount of energy around the persona or situation. The resulting complexes may be a Saviour, a Teacher, an Organizer or a Martyr Complex. We will appear taken over in this role, often oblivious to the hold unless awareness is brought to it by self or by others observing us.

How can you identify your complexes? Due to the strong feeling-toned nature of the complex, a good place to start is to become aware of instances when you are emotionally charged or those times when you seem to be 'taken over' by something. Sometimes complexes take over for a longer period and you may lose libido, feeling depressed or 'in a funk.'

Complexes also act as internal distracters when activated by situations or people associated with the initial complex formation. Thus, they appear unconsciously via misreading words, forgetting or transposing people's names, pausing mid-sentence and other slips-of-the-tongue. The existence of complexes forms the theory behind word association lists used in psychological testing.

In spite of our conscious efforts or intentions, complexes have a life of their own. Carl Jung described the power of complexes in that "complexes can have us." We cannot get rid of complexes yet we can learn how they influence us. Ideally, when we become aware of our complexes, we can at least defuse and shorten their hold on us with the intent of making choices and behaving from a more conscious place.

<u>Reflections</u>

1. When have you felt as if something has 'come over' you? Was it with a certain person, in a certain situation or when you were alone? Try to identify the feeling you were experiencing just before the complex came over you.

    _____

    _____

    _____

    _____

2. What words tend to 'trip you up'? Notice body gestures and voice changes such as slowing down or a raised pitch when talking about certain topics or people. What might psyche be letting you know?

    _____

    _____

    _____

    _____

3. List and name your complexes. Enter into a dialogue with each with the intent of finding out what its needs are.

    _____

    _____

    _____

    _____

4. Mother and Father Complexes are a very common part of our psyches. Contemplate on how you feel and react when talking or thinking about or being in the presence of your parent(s) or with partners. What age do you feel, and what expectations are present?

    _____

    _____

    _____

    _____

5. How does the concept that complexes never go away affect your relationship with your identified complexes?

    _____

    _____

    _____

    _____

Choosing the Hero's Journey

Whether we are viewing *Star Wars* for the tenth time or children are asking us to read *Hansel and Gretel* repeatedly, there is something universally and continuously compelling about these stories. We often feel both deeply energized and content after witnessing them.

One reason for this comfort is that characters in myths and fairytales represent parts of ourselves. As Marion Woodman stated, "at the core of a fairytale is a vision of wholeness." Wholeness or a sense of balance is the ultimate human longing, and the hero enacts the quest for and attainment of this wholeness. As we observe the hero's story, a part of us deeply resonates or associates with his or her experience.

We are all called to the hero's life, yet many of us do not choose to accept this call because we fear giving up the comforts of our lives, positions and ideals. Few choose the hero's journey on their own but rather are forced into it when faced with relationship conflicts, addiction, depression, meaningless, death and other losses. Psyche or soul creates symptoms along with chaos and suffering to move us out of our comfort zone. In these situations, we often have no choice but to cross the threshold into the hero's world.

Like the hero, when we decide to take up this challenge, we are doing something out of the ordinary, something many do not do. Specifically, we begin to observe how we historically and currently act and feel and explore why these ways are no longer working. We soon realize that the quest we have started is not about a distinct endpoint; rather, it is the journey or process of becoming who we are meant to be that is important. As Carl Jung advised, it is the opus—the work on ourselves—that matters.

As we face our inner dragons, we may think, "I wish I had never started"; however, once we are initiated into the hero's journey, a soulful compulsion to live it out drives us, whether we like it or not. As fearful as the journey is, something deep inside us knows that taking the journey is the only real choice. Jung stated that "only one who has risked the fight with the dragon and is not overcome by it wins the hoard, the treasures hard to attain." But what are the dragons?

The ego is frightened by the unconscious ideas, qualities and feelings that threaten its usual way of being. It will defend its habitual, comfortable way of operating by using coping mechanisms such as denial, minimizing, rationalization and avoidance. When we face the inner monsters, however, we gain an understanding of how they have previously influenced our lives. Spending time with our inner beasts results in learning about and incorporating their qualities so they no longer overwhelm us. In the process, we must suffer the losses of once-held beliefs and perceptions of who we are and how we view life.

What about the treasures? The mythic and fairytale heroes find valuable golden eggs and sacred rings. These objects symbolically represent buried past feelings and desires and the potential of our true selves—our real worth. Although we may return from the journey outwardly unchanged, we have begun to heal our inner wounds. We feel increased hope, wisdom, resiliency and creative energy, ready to face another journey when summoned.

Reflections

1. What characters, animals or objects from your childhood stories captured your attention? What qualities of these heroes or items did you admire or wish you had? Imagine yourself having these traits. What would they have allowed you to do or be?

    _____

    _____

    _____

    _____

2. Have you been initiated into the hero's journey? If so, recall how it felt as you crossed the threshold. What fears did you have to overcome in order to continue your quest?

    _____

    _____

    _____

    _____

3. If you have ever faced some of your dragons, what were they? Were they greed, control, feelings of abandonment or something else? When you overcame each dragon, it was not by force or will power, but by a quality of yourself that was summoned. What were the specific traits required?

    _____

    _____

    _____

    _____

4. What is your current relationship with your psychic dragons? Try to identify the quality in you or shift in perception that is being addressed this time?

_____

_____

_____

_____

5. What treasures have you received on your hero's journeys? How have these treasures affected your life since attaining them?

_____

_____

_____

_____

The Cycle of Life

The Christian term *Easter* originated with the pagan Germanic fertility goddess *Eostere*, who had a festival on the Spring Equinox. Her ritual animal was the hare, and she is associated with the full moon and eggs. As much as we associate eggs with fertility, the Easter egg is a symbol of resurrection and new beginnings.

The Easter story speaks to the archetypal pattern of the Eternal Return or the sacrifice-death-rebirth cycle. We see this cycle in the seasons, in the tides and in the phases of the moon. Daily, we sacrifice and consume food to sustain us, eventually returning to the earth ourselves. The forty days of Lent leading up to Easter mark the time of giving up or sacrificing something such as meat or eggs. According to the *Catholic Encyclopedia*, "the real aim of Lent is, above all else, to prepare us for the celebration of the death and Resurrection of Christ."

The sacrifice-death-rebirth cycle has psychological relevance as well. Like the hero's journey, its mythic pattern has purpose in our lives. Joseph Campbell, author of *The Power of Myth,* stated that myths have a pedagogical function of leading us through rites of passage and making the journey from one stage to another with a sense of comfort and purpose. These passages and rites often involve a sacrifice.

The word sacrifice, from *sacra*, means "sacred rites." When we sacrifice, we have a sense of "something given up for the sake of another." Individual sacrifice is necessary to bring forth new energy. This means actively letting go of something of value in service of something larger. On a psychic level, our ego is asked to surrender something—an old attitude or a tired way of seeing our self—in order for something new to emerge.

Folklore stated, "At Easter let your clothes be new, Or else be sure you will it rue." Putting on new clothing symbolically represents the possibility of developing a new aspect of one's identity. It is about letting go and accepting change. As Joseph Campbell advised, "we must let go of the life we have planned, so as to accept the one that is waiting for us." As the cycle indicates, however, change or rebirth does not come without sacrifice or suffering. Jung agreed, stating, "Suffering is necessary for complete development of the psyche" or soul.

This internal letting go is experienced as entering a void, and we fear this darkened space. We fear the losses that will no doubt occur because we have let go. The fear and pain associated with suffering are understandably avoided; however, as the Trappist monk Thomas Merton stated, "the truth that many people never understand, until it is too late, is that the more you try to avoid suffering the more you suffer." We need to be courageous enough to leave behind what was once valued and trust that possibilities more worthy of our true selves will appear.

Spring is a time to reflect on what belief, role or quality you are prepared to let go in order for something new to enter your life. As Helen Keller stated, "character cannot be developed in ease and quiet. Only through the experience of trial and suffering can the soul be strengthened, vision cleared, ambition inspired, and success achieved."

Reflections

1. Recall times when you had to sacrifice a belief or an aspect of yourself. Identify specifically what you were required to let go of? What were the outcomes of this sacrifice? Did something new arise?

    _____

    _____

    _____

    _____

2. Jung stated that "suffering is necessary for complete development of the psyche." How do you define personal suffering? What role do sacrifice and suffering have in your life?

    _____

    _____

    _____

    _____

3. We sometimes symbolically make external changes that often foreshadow psychic change. Look for times when you change your hair, buy new clothes, rearrange the furniture, prune back vegetation and cull the contents of drawers and closets. What do you really want to let go of?

    _____

    _____

    _____

    _____

4. How do you feel about having a void in your life? How well are you able to live with empty drawers, blank walls, and open areas in your home? Are you able to dispose of something without having an immediate replacement for it?

    _____

    _____

    _____

    _____

5. To what extent have you experienced Merton's statement, "The more you try to avoid suffering the more you suffer"?

    _____

    _____

    _____

    _____

Depression Has a Role in Your Life

In the myth, *Inanna*, a descent into the underworld occurs. At each of the seven gates, Inanna is required to surrender a piece of her armour such as her crown, earrings, a double-stranded necklace and breastplate. Symbolically, she has been stripped of aspects of herself such as intellectualizing, her ability to manifest and her female roles. As she lays down her armour, void of the usual means of defending herself, Inanna is alone and helpless, left on a hook as a corpse. She has no choice but to face the depths of her existence.

When people encounter depression, addiction, anxiety or meaningless, they often view their lives as living hell, feeling trapped, caught in the mire, with little or no hope. As unpleasant as these times are, descents provide a passage into our unconscious and offer an opportunity for the reintegration of missing life energy. If we are to gain any renewal, though, we must stay long enough in the angst to learn its wisdom. This belief goes against common practices such as taking anti-depressants or keeping busy to avoid boredom.

Some people voluntarily enter the underworld by recognizing their subtle yearning for 'something more.' For others it takes a profound, "I'm not doing this anymore!" Many times throughout our lives, each one of us enters the dreaded cave, tunnel or watery depths, as Jonah did when swallowed by the whale. As Jung stated, one enters a "tight passage, a narrow door, whose painful constriction no one is spared who goes down to the deep well."

As Inanna experienced, we are required to remove our masks, roles and false persona. We may feel as if we are 'coming apart' or 'going crazy' as we undergo an inner dismemberment. As our fears arise, we ask, "Who am I? How do I really want to live my life?" We find ourselves with outstretched hands, weighing options that no longer have meaning for us.

However stuck in our angst we feel we may be, nothing is ever at an impasse. Energy previously spent outwardly on job, relationships and daily tasks is pulled inward. That energy now goes into trying to problem-solve and into exploring different scenarios and options. As we spend time looking at who we have been and who we want to be, we gain insight into how we have been moving through life. Glimpses of new albeit intimidating possibilities occur.

If we decide to stay in the muck, courageously and patiently holding 'the tension of opposites,' as Jung phrased it, we eventually reach a still point where our perception shifts from old to new. What emerges is neither on one pole or its opposite; it is something else, something new. In adopting the new, we do experience losses, and these bring suffering; however, we are able to handle whatever psyche gives us. As much as the ego is struggling, resisting and suffering, it is strong enough to handle the pain.

As Inanna experienced, we learn that in our moments of powerlessness and hopelessness it is best to turn inward for strength in order to face and accept negative and overused qualities. We eventually reach down and remove the traps we discover have imprisoned us, creating space and energy for the new. We ascend to a new phase of life, integrating the lessons learned in our recent descent. As we continue along the spiral of life, we wisely know there will be other necessary descents that we will heroically accept and journey.

Reflections

1. How do you feel about depression? What associations or reactions arise when you hear people talk about depression? How comfortable are you with people who are depressed?

---

2. How do you handle your own 'funks' or depressed moods? Do you judge them as bad or merely part of the life-death-life cycle? How do you spend your time while 'in the muck'?

---

3. Reflect upon your past descents. What task, whether an action or shift in perspective, was required by you in order for you to ascend from the muck? What parts of you did you have to leave at the gates?

---

4. Can you identify any thoughts or feelings that trigger your descents? Look for patterns of behaviour that foreshadow times of descents.

_____

_____

_____

_____

5. Why do you think descents occur? The Greek god, Hades, as ruler of the underworld, was known as the 'Bringer of all Good Things.' Recall the positive results of your past descents.

_____

_____

_____

_____

Archetypal Influences

Buddha, Christ, Harry Potter and Maggie in the film *Million Dollar Baby* are all examples of the Hero archetype. Their stories follow a shared pattern of stages, such as an unusual birth or childhood, an initiation, an exile, a period of many trials and tests, a symbolic death, a rebirth or transformation, and a return home.

The Hero is a familiar example of an *archetype.* Archetypes are characters, situations and objects in myths, art, literature, religion, and fairytales with which people identify universally. June Singer, author of *Boundaries of the Soul,* suggested that archetypes are "images which help us to organize our life experiences . . . . [They] share a common core with all of humanity."

Warrior, Teacher and Servant, for example, are experienced in most cultures but in different forms. The Warrior archetype appears as G. I. Joe, a Japanese Samurai, Rambo, princess Xena and a Gladiator. Although different, these Warriors all share the common experience of fighting for justice with tenacity and strength. Warriors are usually associated with having a unique attribute, possessing special weapons, and meeting characters that assist their journey.

There are no good or bad, better or worse archetypes. They all bring qualities worthy of incorporating into our lives at certain times. Considering the Rebel archetype, admirable qualities would be challenging authority to evoke social change or rejecting established systems, such as those found in church and family, when they no longer serve us. Rebel energy in a negative manifestation would be rejecting reasonable authority out of anger or merely following others.

Archetypes carry powerful universal themes and emotional meaning such as love and betrayal. Archetypal energy often feels as if something has overtaken us and is possessive and controlling. We may find ourselves in archetypal situations such as living with the Evil Step-Mother or under the wrath of the Tyrannical Father. We may share a similar Orphaned Child story with *Cinderella* or feel as if we are the Outsider, born into the wrong family or not fitting into society, as in *The Ugly Duckling*.

Whether we encounter archetypes in dreams or in the waking world, our psyches are attempting to integrate various qualities into our lives. When we realize we are in a certain negative archetypal pattern, its energy loses some of its hold on us and alerts us to alternate ways of thinking, feeling and acting. Conversely, we can identify archetypes and glean positive attributes from them.

We may be caught in the shadow of the Victim, blaming others and evoking pity in order to get our needs met. In this case, we recognize the Victim role and begin to look at ways to take responsibility for our feelings and actions, and learn ways to be more empowered. We may begin to notice a pattern of falling into the Pioneer shadow, compulsively needing to move or change when stressed. At other times, we may be asked to call up the Hero's outward exploration and respond to challenges.

Like Carl Jung, we can ask, "What myth am I living by?" By looking at archetypes and myth, we gain self-awareness and feel connected to universal themes, compassionately realizing our very human and necessary situation.

Reflections

1. What myth or myths have you lived by? What stories from fairytales, myth, movies and stories are similar to occurrences in your life?

    _____

    _____

    _____

    _____

2. Caroline Myss created a list of 70 archetypes found at http://www.myss.com/library/contracts /three_archs. asp. Peruse the list to acquaint yourself with these archetypes and to look for ones that tend to surface in your life.

    _____

    _____

    _____

    _____

3. From the archetype list, identity archetypes which match the behaviour of people in your life. How might knowing their archetypal tendencies help you relate with them differently?

    _____

    _____

    _____

    _____

4. Write your life or part of it using archetypal situations, characters, items and mythic patterns (e.g., the Hero's journey, the sacrifice-death-rebirth cycle).

_____

_____

_____

_____

5. By what myth might you be living currently? How will you use this knowledge to aid your situation?

_____

_____

_____

_____

Facing Adversity

Have you heard the story about the carrot, the egg and the coffee bean? Well, here is the condensed version. A mother placed a carrot, an egg, and a coffee bean each in a pot of water. After twenty minutes of boiling, she showed her young daughter the results. She explained that each of these objects had faced the same adversity—boiling water—yet each item had reacted differently.

The carrot, although initially strong, hard and unrelenting, had turned soft and weak. The egg, which started fragile, was still protected by its hard outer shell but its inside had hardened. The coffee bean had remained the same yet had changed the water.

So, which one are you? When faced with challenges, pain or even tragedy, how do you react? Are you the carrot, seemingly strong, but with adversity tend to wilt and lose your strength? Perhaps you are more like the egg, starting with a fluid heart but become hardened and tough after a breakup, a financial hardship or some other trial.

Ideally, we would like to face our challenges as the coffee bean did. The bean actually changed the hot water, the very circumstance that brought the pain. It remained true to its self-releasing its unique flavour and fragrance. It literally made the water or situation better.

Perhaps James Hollis was explaining the bean's nature when he wrote, "The measure of our personal development will hinge on two factors: our willingness to accept responsibility for finding our own myth and our ability to sustain the ambiguity that always precedes a new experience of meaning." In order for growth to occur, we must first separate ourselves from the collective by seeking our own path. At the same time, we must deal with the ambiguity around our need for security and control.

Carl Jung stated that "man needs difficulties. They are necessary for health." Problems offer an opportunity for us to look consciously at issues, decisions and solutions. Maintaining a childlike paradisiacal attitude, we often gladly deny or turn away from difficulties. Conversely, we can expand our awareness and consciousness by entering the adversity for a closer look.

Although often hard to imagine, especially when facing the problem in the moment, by embracing the conflict we have an opportunity to see what new and strange aspects of ourselves we are opposing, fearing and wanting to run from. When we maturely face these shadowy traits and viewpoints, a chance for transformation exists.

Jung "learned that all the greatest and most important problems of life are fundamentally insoluble . . . . They can never be solved, but only outgrown." This outgrowing is not solved logically but appears when we detach from childhood ideologies, with a new or transcendent awareness. We are now in a place, as Jung imagined, where "the thunderstorm is still reality, but one is not in it anymore, but above it."

As the coffee bean did with the water, when adversity occurs, it is best to take time to form a relationship with it and to discern what you are being asked to transcend psychically in order to rise above the storm.

Reflections

1. How were challenges faced in your family of origin? Were they looked upon as times to rise to the occasion or as times of suffering? What did you learn from witnessing these reactions?

_____

_____

_____

_____

2. Recall situations where you reacted like the carrot, egg and coffee bean. Which do you tend to behave like most?

_____

_____

_____

_____

3. How willing are you to 'accept responsibility for finding your own myth'? Think of times when you faced adversity, turned inward for the answer and stayed true to your self. What were the results of this way of handling difficulties?

_____

_____

_____

_____

4. How well are you able to 'sustain the ambiguity' of wanting change and yet still holding on to the need for security and control? What childhood ideologies have you had to let go of in order to overcome difficulties?

_____

_____

_____

_____

5. How do you feel about Jung's statement that "man needs difficulties. They are necessary for health."? What advice would you give others about facing adversity?

_____

_____

_____

_____

When Fear Enters Your Life

Whether trying something new, not having heard from family or friends for a while, getting lost while driving, or facing natural disasters, these situations evoke feelings of fear. We experience fear in many forms such as anxiety, worry, doubt, despair, hopelessness, paranoia and even as arrogance and prejudice.

Fear is desired and useful, as it is a source of survival. Fear stimulates a necessary response to danger such as fleeing, hiding or freezing. These reactions are required to keep you safe when facing a traumatic or life-threatening event such as an approaching tsunami, an accident or an abusive situation. Fears that arise regarding such situations are considered rational, as they are based upon real events that require a response in order to avoid threat or to survive.

All other fears, real as they feel, are considered irrational. Upon closer look, they are actually unwarranted or exaggerated and have been triggered by past associations. These fears override or emotionally hijack our higher cognitive brain. We may react with doubt or by aggressively acting out or by turning the media off in avoidance of fear-inducing events or images. What is the source of these irrational fears?

Current research suggests that fears are learned responses to exposure to an event that produces some amount of physical or emotional discomfort. Situations can range from being stung by a wasp to the death of a loved one. We also learn fear indirectly, such as experiencing fear when hearing others tell a horrific story or when witnessing abuse.

Fear has been classified into five types: fear of rejection, fear of the unknown, fear of death, fear of isolation, and fear of the loss of self-dominance or control. As many of these fears overlap, fear is complex. The key is to isolate each of the fears, because fear that is acknowledged is no longer as monstrous as it seems. The discomfort or anxiety that comes from not knowing what the fear is about is what often makes us doubt, worry and fear. Anxiety is unnamed fear.

As with any strong emotion, psyche is speaking, and the fear needs to be examined more closely. Jung stated, "It is a bewildering thing in human life that the thing that causes the greatest fear is the source of the greatest wisdom." Look at the source of your anxiety and fear. Are there some forms of fear that stand out more for you, such as the fear of the unknown or fear of being alone?

Everyone has fears or inner dragons. We cannot avoid them, as they show up in day-to-day life and in our dreams. The poet Fleur Adcock wrote, "It is 5 A.M. All the worse things come stalking in and stand icily about the bed looking worse and worse and worse." What comes visiting you at night? What chases you in your dreams, awakening you in fright? What do you steadfastly avoid doing that would enhance your soul?

Often in the midst of your simple routines, you are called upon to face your fears. Look for these moments of doubt or fear, as fleeting as they may be, and identify the fear. As Jung stated, "only boldness can deliver us from fear, and if the risk is not taken, the meaning of life is violated." Call up your inner hero, approach your fears and take a step towards living your intended life.

Reflections

1. Identify situations which are fear provoking for you. What types of fear occur in these situations? Are there some forms of fear that stand out more for you, such as the fear of the unknown or being alone?

    _____

    _____

    _____

    _____

2. For the most part, you were not born with these fears. Trace back to the origins of these fears. Who taught you about worry, doubting, mistrusting and fear? Give the fear back to the person, realizing you can now function without it.

    _____

    _____

    _____

    _____

3. What does the fear that controls your life cost in terms of your relationships, your community, the world and your soul? Name the losses that occur for you and others when you succumb to your fears.

    _____

    _____

    _____

    _____

4. What do you steadfastly avoid doing? Image yourself actually undertaking this desired action. What voices, thoughts, feelings and fears arise as you consider the possibility of this idea coming into existence?

    _____

    _____

    _____

    _____

5. Dreams or spontaneous daytime images often evoke scary or frightening feelings. Work with these images to gain a better understanding of what you are running from, what trait you are afraid to turn and face, or what you are fearful of letting into your home.

    _____

    _____

    _____

    _____

Why Change Is Difficult

We are familiar with the Greek philosopher Heraclitus' claim that change is the only constant. As much as this is true, we often find change difficult.

We balk or flat-out resist change in a number of ways. We avoid by leaving the room or the relationship when the topic of change comes up. We do anything else but the needed change. We eat or clean, make lists and putter for hours. We rationalize ('It won't work out anyway'), set limitations ('I'm too old'), and use delay tactics ('I'll do it later.') The poet W. H. Auden wrote, "We would rather be ruined than changed; We would rather die in our dread than climb the cross of the present and let our illusions die."

Another way we resist change is by denial. Denial occurs when the psyche literally shuts out what is unbearable or unbelievable. We find ourselves saying, "There's nothing wrong with me" or "It didn't bother you last time." Denial is a defense mechanism for coping with uncomfortable feelings such as anxiety and guilt as we momentarily ponder the change. We have knowledge of what needs to change yet choose not to deal with it.

One of the biggest obstacles to change is fear. Fear of the unknown, of rejection, of lack of control, and of being alone strongly influencing our hesitation. Inner voices say, "What will the neighbours or my family think?" or "I might fail, and then what?"

We spend great amounts of energy hoping and waiting for situations and others to change. We look outwardly instead of inwardly. We blame and make excuses instead of taking responsibility. Writer Leo Tolstoy wrote, "Everyone thinks of changing the world, but no one thinks of changing himself."

How can you evoke a needed change? Start by looking at yourself in the mirror and saying aloud, "I want to change." Notice any hesitations, inner voices talking back, the amount of commitment or your energy level when saying this. What fears, old beliefs and resistances are surfacing? What is in the way?

When we honestly look at what we resist most, we are encountering a source of great learning. The writer Alan Cohen stated, "It takes a lot of courage to release the familiar and seemingly secure, to embrace the new. But there is no real security in what is no longer meaningful. There is more security in the adventurous and exciting, for in movement there is life, and in change there is power."

Trust that with change there will be growth. The political poet Tuli Kupferberg stated, "When patterns are broken, new worlds emerge." There will also be losses, pain and suffering. This is where our fears enter. Recall the sacrifice-death-rebirth cycle. Change and something new cannot occur without a letting go and a loss of some aspect of your self. Change is necessary in life. Be willing to surrender what you are for what you can fully be. Honestly reflect upon what you are afraid to let go.

The writer Geoffrey Madan offered an inspiring image for change: "The dust of exploded beliefs may make a fine sunset." Ah. I wonder what your sunset will look and feel like as you make the necessary changes in your life.

Reflections

1. How well do you handle change? Recount incidents of change accomplished by conscious choice and those that occurred due to outside forces. How did you react in each case?

    _____

    _____

    _____

    _____

2. What are your thoughts on the statement: "There is more security in the adventurous and exciting." What past beliefs, values and attitudes about security surface?

    _____

    _____

    _____

    _____

3. Think of a behaviour or attitude that you currently wish to change. State the wish aloud, as in "I want to change my junk food eating pattern." Notice any hesitations, inner voices, the degree of commitment or your energy level when saying this.

    _____

    _____

    _____

    _____

4. As you contemplate change, what fears, old beliefs and resistances surface? Are the fears realistic? What is the source of these fears or beliefs? What shift in attitude about yourself or others is required from you in order to overcome these fears?

_____

_____

_____

_____

5. Imagine that the change you desire has or is about to happen. How do you feel in this moment of realization? Notice any other voices or feelings that may also be present as the possibility of change nears.

_____

_____

_____

_____

Learning to Make Good Decisions

Although we cannot control or change others or change our histories, we do have some part in what happens in our lives through the choices we make. The word *choice* originates from the Germanic *kausjan*, meaning "to taste, to try" and "to test." *Choice* is also linked to the word *gusto*, with its base *geus*, meaning not only "to taste" or "to choose," but also "to be enjoyed and pleased."

Our task is to make choices more consciously, independent of social, family and peer pressure, detached from unconscious influence established in childhood, and aligned with our true selves.

We make 'bad' choices when, as Carl Jung suggested, our thoughts and feelings are contaminated by past wounds and coping mechanisms. Think of the times when you have felt the consequences of making choices based on ego, pride and fear, or those made against your intuition. "I knew it!" exclaims your true self.

Regardless, you have chosen to act in a manner counter to your values, your beliefs, and your gut, perhaps doing what you think you 'should' do or to please others. Call it karma or trickster energy—something eventually 'bites you in the butt' to remind you to get back on your path.

Sometimes we make choices from a reactionary position. We have swung the pendulum in the opposite direction exclaiming, "I'm never going to be like my mother!" In these situations, we are still not making conscious choices and only see black-and-white options. We have not discerningly asked ourselves, "How do I really want to act in this situation?"

So, how do we begin to make better choices? We stop and assess each situation—sifting, sorting and distinguishing options—taking what we soulfully feel is best for us and leaving what does not.

In the Greek myth, *Psyche and Eros*, Psyche was punished by having to separate a pile of mixed seeds. Faced with this impossible task, Psyche sat still and pondered. In the stillness, an army of ants appeared and helped her complete the task.

Metaphorically, Psyche required the ants—her inner nature—to analyze, sort and select what had been chaotically presented. Like any skill, learning how to best discern takes time, patience and often the ability to wait it out until the 'right' decision arises.

Often it is difficult to make choices because we may not clearly know what we want. Former Secretary-General of the United Nations, Kofi Annan, advised, "To live is to choose. But to choose, you must know who you are and what you stand for, where you want to go, and why you want to get there."

We are not practiced in making choices that best serve our true selves. We were not taught to listen to our bodies, our feelings, our intuition, our dreams, and our desires. We were not taught to value our souls.

Deep down we truly know what is best for us. The writer Robert Louis Stevenson stated, "To know what you prefer, instead of humbly saying Amen to what the world tells you you ought to prefer, is to have kept your soul alive." If we are still enough and put our egos aside, we will hear our bodies and souls whispering, benevolently guiding us to the best choice.

Reflections

1. How do you handle making choices? Do you tend to dread it or get excited? What feelings arise when faced with making choices, whether minor ones (e.g., What's for dinner?) or major ones (e.g., buying a car)?

    _____
    _____
    _____
    _____

2. How does time affect making choices? Do you tend to sleep on it or are you more impulsive? How do you feel about telling yourself or others, "I'll think about that and get back to you."?

    _____
    _____
    _____
    _____

3. Recall the times where you did not listen to your intuition when making a choice. How did the results turn out? Try to remember what deterred you from following your gut?

    _____
    _____
    _____
    _____

4. When we are contemplating a choice, often our body speaks to us. How does your body respond when you are 'off track' or leaning towards an unhealthy choice? It may be your neck, lower back or gastro-intestinal track that lets you know. How does your body respond when you are listening to your gut?

    _____

    _____

    _____

    _____

5. Like the body, dreams reveal what the dreamer is truly feeling about impending or finalized choices. Look for the feeling tone of the dream. Is there a sense of panic, chaos, fear, avoidance or contentment in the dream? Link these feelings to the choice you are facing or have just made.

    _____

    _____

    _____

    _____

Living with Uncertainty

For most people, not knowing an answer and living with uncertainty are difficult situations. We were expected in school to know our lessons. We often were, and may continue to be, reprimanded for saying, "I don't know." In many cases, others, along with our own inner voice, responded back, "What do you mean, you 'don't know?'"

In the case of making a decision such as staying in or leaving a marriage, changing jobs or making a purchase, 'not knowing' means that we are undecided or have not committed fully to an option. Not knowing what to do or having difficulty in making a personal decision can be viewed as an inner conflict. Neither situation nor option feels right. We know we cannot stay if the situation remains the same, yet leaving under the current conditions feels wrong. If only there was an answer to this impasse.

The answer is not this or that, not black-and-white, but instead, it is something other that is most definitely found in the grey palette. Often, when facing conflicting options, we venture into deep, existential and sometimes agonizing issues. Carl Jung stated that "the apparently unendurable conflict is proof of the rightness of your life. A life without inner contradiction is only half a life."

Jung explained this inner contradiction as holding *the tension of opposites*. He noted the worth of this psychic dilemma: "There is no energy unless there is a tension of opposites." When we honour both opposing options, we will find that the answer lies somewhere in between, with a third, more life-enhancing option emerging. This union and integration of the opposites is accompanied by an increase in psychic energy or libido and personal growth.

These painful moments of decision-making allow opportunities for deep personal growth. Jung stated, "Where we most want knowledge is where we are most vulnerable." To live with uncertainty, to hold the tension, and to wait, as uncomfortable as it is, are signs of maturity. If our egos are strong enough to let go of knowing the outcome, making the decisions in the now and being the only part of ourselves that knows the answer, then growth may occur.

Lao Tzu, author of *Tao Te Ching*, asked, "Do you have the patience to wait till your mud settles and the water is clear? Can you remain still enough until the right answer arises by itself?"

Growth comes when the ego experiences a defeat of its usual role of omnipotence and all-knowing. The ego will be asked to acknowledge and take responsibility for previously discarded unconscious material; however, with this loss of ego control comes hope for something new. Jung also said, "The greater the tension, the greater is the potential. Great energy springs from a correspondingly great tension of opposites."

Jung advised, "To risk the not knowing, the ambiguity, is to be free." Begin by giving yourself permission to 'not know.' This creates detachment from either of the opposites and creates room for something else to emerge. Be curious and playful as to how the two options could coexist together. Ask yourself, "What do I really want?" and "How do I want my life to feel?" Trust that the 'right' answer will come when you felt-sense it, often in the form of a dream image, synchronistic situations and with a deeply felt resonance that declares, "Yes, this is it. This is what I want!"

Reflections

1. How well do you live with 'not knowing'? How easy is it for you to say, "I don't know"? What inner voices or bodily sensations emerge during times of not knowing?

    _____

    _____

    _____

    _____

2. Recall times when you did hold the tension and a third option arose. What belief or trait did you have to let go in order for the 'right' option to surface? What did the result of your decision bring in comparison to the two options you were initially contemplating?

    _____

    _____

    _____

    _____

3. As Jung stated, "to risk the not knowing, the ambiguity, is to be free." What do you think the risks are for you? What would the freedom Jung is suggesting look like and feel like for you?

    _____

    _____

    _____

    _____

4. Are you currently holding the tension of opposites? If so, it is helpful to identify the opposites that are battling each other. Dialogue with each of the opposites. What is your ego holding onto and for what reason? What is your soul or heart desiring?

    _____

    _____

    _____

    _____

5. Notice when you soulfully become excited about a seemingly impossible idea or venture. Be aware of ideas casually expressed and then ignored or rationalized. Spend some time with these 'what ifs' and identify beliefs that are hampering further exploration of the ideas.

    _____

    _____

    _____

    _____

Living with Fate

In the film, *Crazy Heart*, Jeff Bridges' character, Bad Blake, referred to doing what he shouldn't do (drinking, multiple failed marriages) as his "fallings." He wisely stated, "It all happens for a reason, even if it's wrong, especially if it's wrong." Blake accepted his fate, even when tragic.

The term *fate* is used to describe whatever is unavoidably given. It is derived from the Latin word *fatum*, meaning "a prophetic declaration, prediction" or "that which is meant-to-be." It also refers to "having been spoken or sentenced by the Gods." Just because it is spoken, however, is it inevitable? How much control or free will do we have in our lives?

Recall the tragedy of *Oedipus Rex*, in which Oedipus is destined by Apollo's oracle to kill his own father and marry his own mother. Even when his parents and Oedipus are told their fate and seek measures to avoid it, predicted events still occur. Oedipus does for the most part act on his own free will. He investigates the murder of Laius, he consults the oracle about the plague, and he forces the truth from the shepherd.

Like Oedipus' life, our lives are often tragic, filled with suffering and mishaps that seem disjointed with our intentions. There can, however, be a positive aspect to our tragedies. As Carl Jung suggested, "the right way to wholeness is made up of fateful detours and wrong turnings." With self-awareness one can begin to see the underlying currents at play in our fateful situations.

Fate includes many factors: genetics, culture, family of origin, personality and unconscious forces. From a psychological perspective, Jung suggested, "When an inner situation is not made conscious, it happens outside, as fate." Elaborating the idea of this unconscious influence, James Hollis suggested that tragedies occur as we make our believed-to-be best choices with our own "wounded vision."

Our unavoidable childhood woundings skew our perceptions of the world and ourselves. We adapt, develop coping mechanisms and unconsciously create personal messages, which surface and influence most of our decisions. We do not knowingly choose abusive partners, addictions, chronic pain, disease, depression or accidents, yet these occur.

Believing that we know who we truly are, what is best for us, and that we have control over situations challenges fate. Hollis wrote, "Puffed by our inflated fantasy of control, we choose our wounded ways, and then have the temerity to curse fate." There is merit to the Rolling Stones' lyrics, "You can't always get what you want, But if you try sometimes you just might find, You get want you need." Similarly, singer-songwriter Jim Cuddy wrote, "Sometimes the world you want is different from the one you find."

Jung advised, "Until you make the unconscious conscious, it will direct your life and you will call it fate." Start by looking at patterns of behaviour in relationships. Identify situations which evoke strong reactions. Look symbolically at body symptoms and dreams. Acknowledge your defense mechanisms. Find a balance between following your intentions and being open to change and opportunities that are presented to you. With enough insight and work, you may *amor fati*—"love your fate."

Reflections

1. How much free will do you feel you have in your life? Over what aspects are you able to have some sense of control? What aspects of your life to you tend to attribute to fate?

_____

_____

_____

_____

2. How do you handle fateful tragedies or, to a lesser extent, events that do not go according to your intentions (e.g., finding a job)?

_____

_____

_____

_____

3. 'You can't always get what you want, but . . . you get what you need.' How do you feel about this statement? Recall times when things did not go your way, and yet the situation later turned out to be better than you expected. What wisdom did you glean from these situations? Are you at the stage of loving your fate?

_____

_____

_____

_____

4. What unpleasant circumstances keep showing up as fate in your relationships, body and emotions? What unfinished business is fate trying to make you address?

    _____

    _____

    _____

    _____

5. What do you think your 'wounded vision' is? What taints your decisions even though ego believes you are making the best decision?

    _____

    _____

    _____

    _____

The Wisdom of Intuition

Call them hunches, gut reactions, intuition or felt-senses—they all provide unique insights into situations. The word *intuition* is derived from the Latin word *intueri*, which means "to look within." According to Mona Lisa Schulz, author of *Awakening Intuition*, intuition "occurs when you directly perceive facts outside the range of the usual five senses and independently of any reasoning process."

Carl Jung defined intuition as "perception via the unconscious." Intuition is a way of perceiving a situation by looking at the whole picture, incorporating history and looking for broad general patterns. Intuition also contemplates the future. It assesses where the current situation might be going. Most importantly, intuition scopes out the possibilities of what you are seeing.

Intuition comes suddenly, is immediate and convincing, and often seems illogical. Occurrences of intuition bring a sense of clarity, truth and absolute indisputability. Intuitive moments or hits have an emotive aspect to them, although the feelings may be difficult to identify. Look for the feeling of empathy; as Schultz stated, "it is often associated with intuition."

Malcolm Gladwell, author of *Blink*, called the part of the brain that leaps to "fast and frugal" conclusions the "adaptive unconscious." He viewed intuitive thought as a "kind of giant computer that quickly and quietly processes a lot of data." According to psychologist Timothy Wilson, the mind delegates a "good deal of high-level, sophisticated thinking to the unconscious . . . [that] does an excellent job of sizing up the world, warning people of danger, setting goals, and initiating action" in an extremely efficient manner. Indeed. Gladwell's studies showed that with merely two seconds of experiencing a situation, you can make decisions just as good as decisions made more deliberately.

You are often told, however, to "take your time" and "think it over." It is rarely acceptable to make a choice without a cognitive reason and certainly not based upon knowing that "it just feels right." You may be ill practiced in using and trusting your intuition and thus may have difficulties in discerning your true intuition from ego-driven, dopamine-filled hopes and expectations. In these situations, taking your time may help you discriminate between ego desires and genuine intuition.

Your body responds in its own unique way during intuitive hits. Sometimes you may feel a tingling sensation or even shivers. According to author Louise Hay, the stomach "digests all the new ideas and experiences we have." It is not surprising that the gut is where you often may feel intuition. As author Deepak Chopra advised, "You can trust your gut feelings a little more because your gut cells haven't yet learned how to doubt their own thinking."

Intuition can be developed and increased. The key is to first acknowledge your intuition and then to begin testing and trusting it. Start by paying closer attention to your whole-body responses to information, people and situations. Deep breathe with specific focus on your core or gut. This fosters greater awareness of this key intuitive area. Keep your mind and body in a relaxed state through diet and body-centered, non-analytical activities such as exercise, yoga, meditation, walks in nature and silence. These create opportunities for your inner wisdom to surface and to be heard.

Albert Einstein stated, "The only real valuable thing is intuition." Learn to trust your intuition. More than once, you have likely been 'bitten-in the butt' when you have not listened to your gut. In these cases, when your ego may have vetoed your intuition, your true self exclaimed, "I knew it." As Jung stated, "The instincts are a far better protection than all the intellectual wisdom in the world."

Reflections

1. Where did you learn to listen (or not listen) to your intuition? What messages did you receive about how to make decisions?

    _____

    _____

    _____

    _____

2. What parts of your body give you intuitive hits? Take five minutes a day to do intentional breathing on your intuitive body area(s). Place your hand on the area and deeply, slowly breathe into it, relaxing the muscles around it. Notice how it feels in this relaxed and receptive state.

    _____

    _____

    _____

    _____

3. How does your intuition speak to you? Identify specific body areas, sensations, thoughts, and 'aha' realizations that are used. Recall past wisdom that has been heard through these means and through dreams.

    _____

    _____

    _____

    _____

4. In what situations do you tend to honour your intuition? In what situations do you have a history of negating your intuition? Why might these situations differ? Try to name exactly what you were not trusting.

    _____

    _____

    _____

    _____

5. How well can you assess a person or situation? Test your intuition by noticing your two-second reaction to something. Compare this to how you were later thinking about the situation or person. Was the initial reaction intuition or ego?

    _____

    _____

    _____

    _____

Abundance Versus Scarcity

As witnessed in the reality show, *Hoarders*, the accumulation of material possessions, especially items deemed worthless, such as yogurt containers, may evoke our wonder as to possible underlying psychologically reasons for such behaviour. When we accumulate or have difficulty in giving, we are working from a scarcity mindset. This worldview assumes a lack of enough success, money, food, friendship, sale items or parking spaces. This attitude manifests in power and control, withholding, stinginess, forcing and the search for security in those who hold it.

Scarcity mentality believes in a win-lose situation that isolates people and establishes me-you and us-them camps. A sense of comparing and competition is established by those who hold this view, and they often relate to others from a position of what they can get from them. Scarcity-based people believe, "Don't trust anyone; they're out to get you" and "Don't get too attached to something or someone as you'll probably lose it."

Despite having enough and knowing we are capable of getting more, we may have a feeling that the good will not last and may persistently want more. These scarcity-driven attitudes and behaviours are symbolic of deeply feeling that we are not good enough. We cope by taking an attitude that life is about struggle, competition, and grasping for items and experiences to boost our egos. As Gary Zukav, author of *Seat of the Soul*, noted, "scarcity of self value cannot be remedied by money, recognition, affection, attention or influence."

The opposite of a scarcity is abundance. The worldview of abundance is based upon the principle that there is enough for everyone. It is based on an attitude of generosity, patience, trust, and letting go of security and control. We deeply feel we have enough and wholeheartedly believe "I am enough."

A belief in abundance relies heavily upon the principle of interconnectedness. As author of the book, *The Trance of Scarcity*, Victoria Castle stated, "an abundance paradigm views the world in terms of boundless potential, where there is the possibility of enough for everyone." When we work from an attitude of abundance, we rejoice in the successes of others, knowing that we have and will continue to achieve our own successes. Author Stephen Covey suggested we take an attitude of believing that other people's success "adds to . . . rather than detracts from . . . our lives."

We learn about scarcity and abundance in childhood. If we experienced childhoods in which our physical, emotional or psychological needs were unmet, we received the message that there is 'not enough.' Conversely, with 'good enough' parenting, where our needs were met to some level of healthy childhood ego development, we learned to trust that our needs will be met and tend to feel we are 'good enough.' We develop early an abundance or scarcity complex that relates to seeing the world through an optimistic or pessimistic lens.

Some people may argue that a worldview of abundance requires a utopian vision; however, it actual reveals scarcity as a shadow quality. Using the example of world hunger, Castle argued that, "World hunger is not a result from a dearth of food, it's a product of national and global policies rooted in greed and scarcity." Indeed. We also need to be conscious of the realms in which we are abundant. Franklin Roosevelt wisely stated, "The test of our progress is not whether we add to the abundance of those who have much. It is whether we provide enough to those who have little."

Reflections

1. What attitude do you tend to work from—abundance or scarcity? Consider your ability to be generous, as with tipping or volunteering your time or service.

    _____

    _____

    _____

    _____

2. How easy is it for you to donate or let go of items? What fears are evoked when contemplating letting go and trusting that the universe will provide more?

    _____

    _____

    _____

    _____

3. Reflect upon Covey's statement that other people's success 'adds to' your life. Where have you experienced this occurring?

    _____

    _____

    _____

    _____

4. Lao Tzu stated, "He who obtains has little. He who scatters has much." How do you feel when you 'scatter' your belongings, money and time?

_____

_____

_____

_____

5. Find the source of your scarcity or abundance. What messages did you receive in childhood about where and how to be generous or withholding?

_____

_____

_____

_____

The Importance of Gratitude

The philosopher Eric Hoffer stated, "The hardest arithmetic to master is that which enables us to count our blessings."

Gratitude is a virtue disposing the mind to an inward sense and an outward acknowledgment of a gift or benefit received. Gratitude is the appreciation of what is valuable and meaningful to you and represents a general state of thankfulness, gratefulness or appreciation. Gratitude encompasses abundance, simple appreciation, appreciation of others and the world, optimism, life satisfaction, hope, spirituality/religiousness, forgiveness, empathy and prosocial behavior. It is negatively related to depression, anxiety, materialism and envy.

Gratitude has one of the strongest links with mental well being of any character trait. Research has measured improvements in mood, specifically depression, when practicing gratitude. Such benefits include better physiological health (heart rhythms and sleep patterns), fewer physical symptoms (headaches, colds), increased performance at work (cognitive functioning), higher states of alertness, determination and energy, and an increased sense of connectedness to others.

Gratitude is also a readiness to return or express the gift or feeling of appreciation. As writer William Arthur Ward noted, "Feeling gratitude and not expressing it is like wrapping a present and not giving it." Expressions of gratitude by one person tend to motivate others to express gratitude. Showing gratitude thus initiates a virtuous cycle, enhancing positive reciprocal behavior. Indeed, gratitude when shared with others has significant effects. Psychologist Robert Emmons of the University of California Davis found, "When we express an emotion, it tends to magnify or amplify the feeling. So expressing thanks makes our gratitude stronger."

Expressing gratitude also strengthens relationships. What is good for the giver of gratitude is also good for the person receiving it. Research showed that the expression of thanks "more than doubled the likelihood that helpers would provide assistance again."

Gratitude can be introduced into your day by saying "thank you," sending thank-you notes telling people what you appreciate about them, identifying in the moment what you are appreciating (the sky, a smell, a touch, a pen), accepting compliments and gifts from others working from an attitude of abundance rather than scarcity and regularly using a gratitude journal. Rejoice in or appreciate even the small things. This could be as simple as finding a single paper clip that although not necessarily vital, surely adds to the flow of your task.

As with any trait, gratitude has its opposite trait, envy, which needs to be recognized in your life. If gratitude is fearless, then envy is full of fear and steeped in the scarcity principle of 'not enough.' Your envy can even be directed toward yourself, showing up as that inner voice that enviously prevents you from believing in and pursuing your dreams. It says, "You're too old, not smart enough, don't have enough money" to manifest your hopes. Try to identify the source of these inner pronouncements.

You learn gratitude at an early age. Psychoanalyst Melanie Klein suggested that gratitude is associated with trust in good people. This trust is established in childhood when the infant has received a desired gift from a loved one (e.g., satiation with food, mirrored feelings), feels full gratification, and has integrated without greed or envy the enjoyment from obtaining the gifts. Gratitude and a sense of feeling fully understood have been established. These internal states form the basis of inner worth, generosity and unity in future relationships.

Reflections

1. Take the quick and user-friendly six-question Gratitude questionnaire found online at http://psychology. ucdavis.edu/Labs/PWT/Image/emmons/file/GQ-6-scoring-interp_08_10_11.pdf. How do you feel about your score and its meaning?

_____

_____

_____

_____

2. Without repeating any item previously listed, write a list of five items that you are grateful for having in your life. Do this every day for three weeks.

_____

_____

_____

_____

3. Sometimes you do not see all that you can be grateful for in your life. Look around and imagine your life without certain people and items. This exercise can also be applied to past and current situations.

    _____

    _____

    _____

    _____

4. When you are thinking about each gratitude, note any hesitancy, feelings and body gestures. Might some of these gratitudes be forced? Are these true gratitudes or are they obligated or indebted feelings of owing someone thanks?

    _____

    _____

    _____

    _____

5. Where does your envy appear? Is it directed at others' possessions, travels or relationships? What part of you envies another part of yourself? What fears lie behind the envy?

    _____

    _____

    _____

    _____

Afterwards

Soul Reflections has introduced you to some of the basic concepts of depth psychology and has brought increased awareness to the inner world of your unconscious. It is simply a beginning, one part in your journey. Yoga, meditation, and bringing mindfulness to all of your activities can enhance the stilling of ego's incessant thoughts and allow unconscious wisdom to enter your awareness. With improved awareness comes the ability to make better decisions in all areas of your life. I invite you to revisit certain chapters when faced with similar life situations and to enrich your understanding by perusing some of the books in the bibliography.

Bibliography

Campbell, Joseph, with Bill Moyers. *The Power of Myth*. Edited by Betty Flowers. New York: Anchor Books, 1991.

Castle, Victoria. *The Trance of Scarcity: Stop Holding Your Breath and Start Living Your Life*. San Francisco: Berrett-Koehler Publishers, 2006.

Estés, Clarissa Pinkola. *Women Who Run With the Wolves: Myths and Stories of the Wild Woman Archetype*. New York: Ballantine Books, 1992.

Hollis, James. *The Eden Project: In Search of the Magical Other*. Toronto: Inner City Books, 1998.

————— *Creating a Life: Finding Your Individual Path*. Toronto: Inner City Books, 2000.

————— *What Matters Most: Living a More Considered Life*. New York: Gotham Books, 2009.

Johnson, Robert A. *Inner Work: Using Dreams & Active Imagination for Personal Growth*. San Francisco: Harper & Row, 1986.

Jung, C.G. *Man and His Symbols*. New York: Dell Publishing, 1968.

_____ *Modern Man in Search of a Soul.* Oxford: Routledge, 2001.

Hay, Louise. *You Can Heal Your Life,* gift ed. Carlsbad, CA: Hay House, 1999.

Maté, Gabor. *When The Body Says No: Understanding the Stress-Disease Connection.* Hoboken, New Jersey: John Wiley & Sons, Inc., 2003.

_____ *In the Realm of Hungry Ghosts: Close Encounters with Addiction.* Toronto: Vintage Canada, 2008.

Mellick, Jill. *The Art of Dreaming: Tools for Creative Dream Work.* Berkeley, CA: Conari Press, 2001.

Moore, Thomas. *Care of the Soul: A Guide for Cultivating Depth and Sacredness in Everyday Life.* New York: HarperCollins, 1992.

Neumann, Erich. *Depth Psychology and a New Ethic.* Boston: Shambhala, 1990.

Schultz, Mona Lisa. *Awakening Intuition: Using Your Mind-Body Network for Insight and Healing.* New York: Three Rivers Press, 1998.

Singer, June. *Boundaries of the Soul: The Practice of Jung's Psychology.* New York: Anchor Books, 1972.

Woodman, Marion. *Addiction to Perfection: The Still Unravished Bride.* Toronto: Inner City Books, 1982.

Woodman, Marion, and Elinor Dickson. *Dancing in the Flames: The Dark Goddess in the Transformation of Consciousness.* Toronto: Knopf Canada, 1997.

Young-Eisendrath, Polly, and Terrence Dawson (Eds.). *The Cambridge Companion to Jung.* Cambridge: Cambridge University Press, 1997.

Zukav, Gary. *The Seat of the Soul.* New York: Simon & Schuster, 1989.

About the Author

Diane Hancox is a depth psychotherapist, speaker and writer living in Parksville, British Columbia, Canada. She obtained a M.A. in Counselling Psychology (with emphasis in Depth Psychology) from Pacifica Graduate Institute. Her weekly column, "The Joy of Being Jung," appears in the *Oceanside Star.* Her work offers an integrative, insightful and practical way of approaching the unconscious with the intent of enriching the lives of people ready to make a shift in personal consciousness.

Look for *Soul Reflections, Volume 2* in late 2012. For more information go to http://www.corecounselling.ca